RHYTHM AND FREE VERSE
ACROSS THE SLAVIC BELT

RHYTHM
AND
FREE VERSE
ACROSS THE
SLAVIC BELT

Selected and Translated by

DASHA C. NISULA

EXILE
e d i t i o n s

singular fiction, poetry, nonfiction, translation, drama, and graphic books.

Library and Archives Canada Cataloguing in Publication

Title: Rhythm and free verse across the Slavic belt / selected and translated by
   Dasha C. Nisula.
Names: Nisula, Dasha Čulić, editor, translator.
Description: Includes bibliographical references.
Identifiers: Canadiana (print) 20230484042 | Canadiana (ebook) 20230484158 |
   ISBN 9781550969375 (softcover) | ISBN 9781550969382 (EPUB) |
   ISBN 9781550969399 (Kindle) | ISBN 9781550969405 (PDF)
Subjects: LCSH: Slavic poetry—Translations into English. | LCSH: Slavic poetry—
   History and criticism.
Classification: LCC PG551.E3 R49 2023 | DDC 891.808—dc23

Translation Copyright © Dasha C. Nisula, 2023
Book and cover designed by Michael Callaghan
Cover artwork © Marko Marian
Typeset in Baskerville font at Moons of Jupiter Studios

Published by Exile Editions ~ www.ExileEditions.com
   144483 Southgate Road 14, Holstein, Ontario, N0G 2A0
Printed and Bound in Canada by Gauvin

We gratefully acknowledge a financial contribution from Western Michigan University.

Canadian sales representation: The Canadian Manda Group, 664 Annette Street,
Toronto ON M6S 2C8 www.mandagroup.com 416 516 0911

North American and international distribution, and U.S. sales:
Independent Publishers Group, 814 North Franklin Street,
Chicago IL 60610 www.ipgbook.com toll free: 1 800 888 4741

In memory of
Conrad Hilberry

EAST SLAVIC BELT / RUSSIA · 39
SELECTED FROM EARLY 20TH THROUGH 21ST CENTURY WORKS

VLADIMIR BURICH ~ Selections from various collections

VYACHESLAV KUPRIYANOV ~ Selections from various collections

Armstrong

Black angel
announcing the end of the Harp

Prometheus
bound to the trumpet

—Vladimir Burich

Introduction to Slavic Free Verse
by
Dasha C. Nisula

Before deliberate exports of mass-cultural icons including Coca-Cola, (introduced to East Europeans after World War II), fast-food restaurants such as McDonald's, Pizza Hut, and Subway (introduced in the 1990s), America had unwittingly exported two quintessential American art forms: jazz and modernized free verse. Interestingly enough, both of these cultural exports were not well received in America of the late 19th and early 20th centuries, and neither were they sent abroad with cheers and hopes of growth and expansion, as was the case with economic exports. In fact, neither free verse, introduced in its modern form by Walt Whitman, nor syncopated music, played in Europe by early African American jazz ensembles, were well accepted on the American soil. It is only once these artistic forms received a positive reception on the European continent, where they were appropriated to different degrees, that these genuine American forms return home to receive the recognition they deserve on their native soil.

This is not to say that free verse and syncopated music had an easy time in Europe, either in Victorian England or especially in Central and East Europe, where socialist and repressive governments controlled artistic expression and did not approve of such bourgeois tendencies. While there was a minority in the British Isles that hoped for change and a move toward modernism, in Central and East Europe the people were pushing for national independence, revolution, and freedom from repressive regimes that held their cultural life in check. This was especially true for the last decades of the 19th and first decades of the 20th century.

But how free verse and jazz survived Russian revolutions, two major World Wars, and oppressive socialist and communist systems, is a study that has yet to be completed. May this material serve as an impetus to those who might be interested in exploring this rich and inexhaustible topic. The focus here will be on the embrace and spread of free verse and jazz across the Slavic belt of South-Central and East Europe. In this study I posit that American poetry of Walt Whitman, based on the principle of complete freedom, and American music of African American jazz players influenced the artistic world from the most Western part of Europe to its most Eastern part, across the dominant Slavic cultural belt that spans the European continent.

Looking at the trajectory that links West Europe, East Europe, and America, it begins at the dawn of industrial age in mid-19th century Russia. Author Fyodor Dostoevsky turned his back toward the industrial progress made by man, when not even a fraction of that progress could be applied to the change in human behavior. In the figure of the Underground Man, he stuck his tongue out at the Crystal Palace displayed in London in 1851, though he himself said he could not even do that. Another man, miles away and responding to his own local Crystal Palace in New York, Walt Whitman had quite a different response. Mesmerized by the fusion of art and science, he not only embraced the Crystal Palace of 1853 but used it as a metaphor for the kind of art and influence he, and America as a whole, would have upon the world that would follow. Indeed, though he was known to have advanced the popularity of free verse, Walt Whitman could not have even dreamed about the impact his style and *Leaves of Grass* would have not only upon the generations of writers in his own land but across the sea in Europe.

And what made American cultural exports so attractive to the Europeans, especially East Europeans of the 20th century, is the fact that both represented fluidity and freedom of expression, expectation, and optimism that were dominant at the dawn of the 20th century, and after the exhausting tragedy of the two World Wars on the European continent. What African American music offered was a release, enjoyment in human participation in the body politic, while free verse represented hope for something more than meter and rhyme, a free and spontaneous expression of inner human experiences.

We know that in most cultures one can find early forms of free verse writing that appear in scriptural form in their own early texts. But American free verse, and specifically Whitman's who modernized and popularized it, hit the European continent from England in the last decades of the 19th century. And it was in England that Whitman first received recognition for his work *Leaves of Grass*, and admiration by Lord Tennyson and Robert Louis Stevenson. The first British edition of Whitman's work was selected and edited by William M. Rossetti in 1868. Subsequently, his verse traveled eastward to France and Germany, European artistic and cultural centers, across the Slavic belt through Central Europe and to Russia in the far eastern part of Europe.

The first among Slavs to mention Walt Whitman's name in 1861 were the Russians. At that time East Europeans knew very little about Walt Whitman and the general readership, even the educated public, did not have good enough command of English to read Whitman in the original, or even understand what Whitman was trying to say in *Leaves of Grass*. However, once his work reached England and was well received, the news about a new revolutionary poet in America, who embraced not only the modern industrial age but offered a new modern form of expression in free verse, traveled quickly to Central and East Europe, where people were beginning to read Whitman before the 1905 aborted Russian Revolution. In fact, an article on Whitman was published in Poland in 1887, and in Russia one of the first admirers of Whitman was Ivan Turgenev, a prose writer who in the early 1870s spent some time in Paris and acquainted himself with Whitman's work and was going to translate it. He was especially moved by Whitman's *Beat! Beat! Drums!* So by the end of the 19th century, Walt Whitman's poetry was already familiar among Russian writers. And by the early 20th century, Russian Futurists were already writing in Whitmanesque style.

In addition, Leo Tolstoy became familiar with Whitman's work, after receiving a copy of Whitman's book. He urged that the work be translated; however, it was not until the beginning of the 20th century, in 1903, that Konstantin Balmont began to translate Whitman and published his translations in 1905. Not knowing English, he relied heavily on his wife's prose translations which he subsequently versified. This approach certainly contributed to Russian's misunderstanding of Whitman's work and calling it not really poetry but rhythmic prose. Errors in translation of *Leaves of Grass* complemented errors about Whitman's work that go back to 1861 when his work was referred to as a novel. Other errors came with the list of the dates of his death, and even his name appeared in different forms as Valt Vitman, or Uot Uitmen.

However, the best translation of *Leaves of Grass* into Russian was made by Kornei Chukovsky with the very first poem he translated in 1902. A scholar and translator, Chukovsky was the pioneer booster for Whitman in Russia. The political and social climate was ripe with revolutionary fever and his work was immediately translated and read by Russians. The most popular hit of Whitman's poetry was Chukovsky's "Beat! Beat! Drums!" a translation used primarily as propaganda material for Red troops to spur them on to the revolutionary spirit that was to spread across the country in the early part of the 20th century. Whitman's influence here was rather political than poetical. Pointing out inexcusable errors in Balmont's translations of Whitman, Kornei Chukovsky published his own translations in the Russian satirical magazine *Signal*. Chukovsky's work was censored as early as 1905, while articles on Whitman published in Russia were censored by the czar's censors even in the 1880s. Chukovsky's first edition of *Leaves of Grass* appeared in print in 1907, one year after the Czech translation of *Leaves of Grass* came out in 1906, translated by several poets, among them Jaroslav Vrchlický who had begun translating Whitman as early as 1895. With the two translations of *Leaves* in major Slavic languages, and the 1909 complete *Leaves of Grass* in French, along with articles and poems in periodicals, writers and the reading public in Central and East Europe certainly knew about Walt Whitman.

The European avant-garde that first began in the graphic arts was already strong in Russia by the first two decades of the 20th century. In

1915 Kazimir Malevich painted his "The Black Square" symbolizing the break with object and figure in art. By the 1917 Russian revolution, Whitman was highly praised. He was glorified as the poet of the revolution, of new democracies, unity of people and brotherhood of all nations. Russian Futurists sought liberation of language, art and life from tradition and convention. Interested in innovation, they began to appropriate Whitman's form of modern versification, as we can note in the works of such poets as Alexander Blok, Velimir Khlebnikov, Vladimir Mayakovsky and Marina Tsvetaeva. In 1918 Sergey Esenin's collection *Transformation* came out in print. Life for these poets was not an easy one. Khlebnikov died in 1922 at the age of 37, while Esenin and Mayakovsky died by suicide also in their 30s, and Tsvetaeva in her late 40s.

After that initial exposure to free verse from abroad and domestic poets, Russia's poetic creativity took a back seat to all the political turmoil the country was experiencing: First World War, Russian Revolution of 1917, followed by the Civil War, and decades of regulations on the creative processes of writers, artists, and musicians. There was a period of relaxation, however, during the 1920s, a period known as NEP, when New Economic Policies were introduced to uplift the social and economic atmosphere in the country. Loosening of censorship occurred in all the arts and on the economic front. New opportunities opened doors to entertainment and artistic endeavors. As the country began to recover, so did the human spirit awaken with the help of music from the West, modern dance, and rhythms of American oral tradition, jazz. And in the early 1920s, publishing of Walt Whitman in Polish translation began by a number of poets as Stanisław de Vincenz, Tadeusz Grzebieniowski, Alfred Tom, and Stefan Stasiak among others.

Just as many individuals from Central Europe ended up in West European cultural centers at the beginning of the 20th century, so did many Russian artists and writers. One of them was Valentin Parnakh who in the early 1920s attended the Sorbonne in Paris. He wrote many articles on modern artistic developments in music and the performing arts. Some of these were published in West Europe where he also visited

Russian communities. In 1919 his book of poems *SAMYM* was published in Paris. In the same year he heard Louis Mitchell's *Jazz Kings* in Paris and was the first to introduce the word jazz (джаз) to the Russian language. As an early Russian jazz advocate, he introduced jazz and a series of new dances to Soviet audiences. In his book *History of Dance*, published in Paris in 1932, he points out the similarities among early primitive dances from across many different cultures. He includes the Orient, Spain, Africa and Isadora Duncan, the American modern dance pioneer, who visited Russia and Poland in the early part of the 20th century and, in 1922, married the Russian poet Sergey Esenin. Syncopated music Parnakh claimed isn't only featured in jazz but in ancient languages such as Sanskrit and Hebrew. He defines syncopation as an ancient element common to music, language, and movement which transformed and in the 20th century appears in its new form in free verse, music, dance, and drama. Russian musical heritage and theatrical arts during this period were open to jazz. Once forbidden styles and techniques were adopted and ragtime exuberance ruled in Soviet life. Igor Stravinsky had a passion for jazz and incorporated ragtime in his "Firebird" Suite, written for the 1910 Paris season of Sergei Diaghilev's *Ballets Russes*. In the mid-1920s Russian composer Dmitri Shostakovich was moved by jazz and orchestrated "Tea for Two."

By the end of the 1920s, the Communist Party put an end to this invasion of unacceptable, foreign, degenerate music and behavior. In the next decade, the atmosphere changed completely once Joseph Stalin was the head of the former Soviet Union. In the mid-1940s, when World War II ended, there was a sense of relief, but the country as a whole was destroyed as was the human spirit. That was true not only for East but West Europe as well. And then by the early 1950s, and especially after Stalin's death in 1953, followed by Khrushchev's denunciation of Stalin in 1956, discussions on the creative process began again. Creative minds wanted to pick up the links with pre-war artistic trends. Interest in not only jazz but in free verse once again surfaced among East and West European artists, musicians, poets, and the general public.

A similar awakening that appeared in Russia after World War II also took place on the West end of the Slavic belt that runs through Central Europe, among former Warsaw Pact countries, and in the former Yugoslavia, though the socialist realist hand held firmly on to the creative processes. Looking at the Western end, an article about Whitman by Milan Marjanović was published in Serbia in 1897, and in the same year Whitman was mentioned in a Slovenian journal, *New Hope*. But the first translations of Whitman into Slovenian by Tone Seliskar appeared in print in an American Slovenian publication of 1926. In Croatia, first translations appeared in print in *Svjetlo* (*Light*) in 1900 by an anonymous translator who had a rough time with the "strange rhythm of irregular lines," and in 1904 Whitman was mentioned in a Zagreb publication, *Pictures from the History of English Literature*. By 1909, first translations of German poets and Whitman's poems in Croatian and Serbian appeared in the Bosnian review *Bosanska Vila*, a publication that was introducing South Slavs to the work by Walt Whitman.

The very first Croatian free verse poems belong to Vladimir Jelovšek who, as early as 1898 and 1900, was influenced by foreign modern innovations. But it was a young man by the name of Janko Polić Kamov who made the most significant mark in the development of verse in Croatia in just a decade of writing during his short life of 24 years. The most critical work is his shocking first collection, *Psovka* (*Curse*), published in 1907. He belonged to a pre-avant-garde group that, in the first decade of the 20th century, turned all the conventions in Croatian literature upside down. The group was very close to the French, Italian, and Spanish developments in literary and artistic worlds of the time. Kamov, a pseudonym taken from the Biblical son Kam, who exposed the nakedness of his father, had a goal to undermine the social value system, proposing a new style in prose very close to the manifesto of Futurism proposed in 1909. In fact, he is known as the first Futurist who rejected all contemporary norms of verse, prose and drama and is considered as the precursor of the avant-garde period in Croatian letters. He incorporated the Biblical tradition of free verse in his poem "Song of Songs" in order to expose human spiritual nakedness. Though he died young in 1910, he left a few significant pieces for the new generation of writers.

As World War I devastated the country and the whole of Europe, in the city of Zagreb, culturally close to Prague and open to news from East and West, we find another young poet Antun Branko Šimić already writing and publishing his free verse in 1917. His full collection *Preobraženja* (*Transformations*) was published in 1920, and his poem "My Transformations" begins with a line: *One's self I sing*. His work represents known transcendental idealism and his verse makes a complete break with conventional forms. His focus in the collection is on expressionistic rhythm. He must have been acquainted with Walt Whitman, as evidenced in the only book published during his lifetime. With his literary, theoretical and critical views, poems in *Preobraženja* appear as new and fresh poetry in which he allows his poetic expression to take the color of a speaking voice, focusing on sound, internal rhythm, and repetition. He wrote the way he felt. In this volume, he brought free verse into Croatian literature, completely abandoning punctuation, with a focus on visual representation of the text. Unfortunately, just like Kamov, Šimić died young in 1925 in his 20s, leaving behind several very significant works. And just like Kamov, he established important groundwork for the writers to come.

Another important figure in the development of free verse in Croatia is that of Augustin Ujević, known as Tin Ujević. He corresponded with Šimić and was active as a poet before World War I and after World War II. He was very productive, engaging in similar ideas as Kamov and Šimić, stressing innovation in poetry. Tin Ujević was a wanderer most of his life and traveled a lot, seeking new inspiration, and spent five years in Paris from 1914 to 1919. There he was exposed to writers from the West and the East and was introduced to major world literary figures. Upon his return to Zagreb, he began writing in new forms. Already a master of classical verse (see his sample written in 1916 in Paris), his third collection published in the mid-1920s contained poems in free verse. As a prolific writer, he published a number of books during the 1930s, and then there was yet another war. Many social and political changes took place in what was to become former Yugoslavia after World War II. Because of his leftist ideas and former political stance, the new Communist regime did not allow Ujević to publish his works during the 1940s. He devoted himself to translation, as have many other poets in the region.

Two other poets who engaged in translation and began publishing in the 1930s were Dragutin Tadijanović and Drago Ivanišević. A classical poet, Tadijanović was influenced by the Biblical style, folk poetry, and Šimić, focusing on the human condition with precise use of language. Ivanišević's first poems were in prose, but he mostly published in free verse, employing rhythm and free association. He was well-acquainted with the work of French, Spanish and Italian modernists and translated Federico García Lorca into Croatian.

A poet of leftist ideas and an interest in innovation, Jure Kaštelan spent some time as a lecturer at the Sorbonne and was exposed to modern trends. He completed his first book *Crveni konj* (*Red Horse*) in 1940. The content of the book and the poems' messages were not approved by the censors, and the book was suppressed and destroyed. Then, as soon as World War II ended, a young poet, Vesna Parun, managed to publish her first book *Zore i Vihori* (*Dawns and Hurricanes*) in 1947. The book contained free verse and came from a young woman full of life after a devastating war, writing about her own feelings and experiences, something that was not encouraged by the tightly controlled Writers' Union. She was immediately reprimanded. In the same year, translations of Walt Whitman appeared in print in Bulgaria and Poland.

Another post-World War II book, published in 1950 in then Yugoslavia, was Tin Ujević's *Rukovet* (*Handful*), edited by Jure Kaštelan. In the same year Kaštelan's own book was published, *Pijetao na krovu* (*Rooster on the Roof*), which already displayed a Whitmanesque style. The following year, in 1951, Ujević's translation of Walt Whitman's *Leaves* of Grass (*Vlati trave*) appeared in print. Then with the first of his four collections published in the 1950s, Slavko Mihalić made his literary debut with *Komorna muzika (Chamber Music)* in 1954. This first small collection consisted of 12 poems, the same number as the first collection of Walt Whitman's *Leaves of Grass*.

By the early 1950s, the population of East Europe was in dire need of recuperation, following the devastation World War II left all across the European peninsula. Not only the land, but the social fabric and the peoples' spiritual health were in need of some sort of uplifting. Nothing could accomplish this better than what C.K. Williams calls: "Whitman's unpredictable music," the language of free verse and the openness and all-inclusive oral tradition of syncopated music of jazz, played the way the musician felt. Artistically speaking, the 1950s were extremely important among socialist countries in Central and East Europe. A Czech translation of Whitman's *Leaves of Grass* by Jiří Kolář and Zdeněk Urbánek was published in 1955; and a Slovak translation of *Pozdrav svetu (Salut au monde)* by Ján Boor and Magda Seppová in 1956. That same year Drago Ivanišević's translations of African and African American poetry appeared in print. And by the late 1950s, most of the East European population was eagerly listening to American jazz played regularly over Voice of America.

As European countries were recovering, the trajectory of East/West Europe and America began to shift, and, during the second half of the 20th century it was America that was the focus in this trajectory. Indeed, after World War II, Europe was desolate; many excellent minds left the old continent in search of new more fruitful grounds and came to the United States. Where before World War II America was behind Europe in following artistic trends, after the war America – unique, new and different – began to assert itself as a superpower on political and economic terms. As such it had to claim the position on aesthetic terms as well. And it seems that Clement Greenberg brought this about with the New York School of Abstract Expressionism and artists including Jackson Pollack, Willem de Kooning, and Mark Rothko.

It is interesting to note that, just as free verse and jazz did not have an easy entry in Europe, in the second half of the 20th century free verse and jazz were of great interest among the East and West European writers, musicians, scholars, and students, as much in all of Europe as in the United States. Free verse today is one of the most popular modes of expression among Russian youth. In fact, there are now annual free verse festivals being held in Moscow and Saint Petersburg, in Siberia, and in other towns across the country. Publications of collections of free verse and selections from annual festivals are readily available to the reading public, as are numerous poetry sites on the internet.

Though free verse in Russia is only now beginning to be fully appreciated, the development of Russian free verse from the beginning of the 20th century to post-Stalinist period took courage. Writers not only experienced difficulties and took risks while engaging in such experimental (imported) forms, but they also went through periods of severe government censorship and had to endure years of writing without being published in their homeland. Those who did not meet the official party ideology were silenced and lost their professional status. There was an atmosphere under which talented writers were unable to fully realize their talents. Some of them began publishing in samizdat known as "unofficial" literature. One such journal, *Sintaksis*, printed new and unpublished young poets of the 1950s and 1960s.

Two writers who made some of the most important contributions, not only in their practical writing of free verse but also in their theoretical and critical assumptions on prosody in post-Stalinist Russia, are Vladimir Burich and Vyacheslav Kupriyanov. Because both of these poets had a hard time publishing in their country, they have an extensive record of translating poetry from other languages into Russian. Burich translated from other Slavic languages such as Czech poets, and the Polish poet Tadeusz Różewicz; Kupriyanov translated Austrian, German, and American poets, Walt Whitman and Carl Sandburg. Their own writing in free verse had to wait to finally appear in print in Russia: Kupriyanov's came out in 1981, while Burich's first book appeared in 1989. As a result, both of these writers are known in other European countries and they have been recognized by literary organizations, having received numerous awards. Vladimir Burich was first published in France and Poland, while Mr. Kupriyanov's poetry and prose are especially well known and respected in Germany. There is also one collection of his verse that has appeared in English translation, *In Anyone's Tongue*, published in 1992.

Burich is Russia's Whitmanist, a sword in defense of free verse, cutting a line to its bare essence, and Kupriyanov is the shield. Both have made considerable contributions to the development and understanding of free verse in Russia. In an interview by Aleksandar Lukić in Požarevac, Serbia on October 14, 1990, Vladimir Burich points out that he also began as a syllabo-tonic writer and that his teacher, a reformer Vladimir Mayakovsky, opened that syllabo-tonic cage and freed him to write the way he feels. Burich helped organize the very first Free Verse Festival in the coal mining center of Leninsk-Kuznetsky in Siberia in 1986, followed by the second in Kaluga, sponsored by the famous eye surgeon Dr. Fyodorov, and the third festival in Moscow. A collection of four poets, two of which were Burich and Kupriyanov and titled *White Square*, Part I, was published in Moscow in 1988 by Prometheus. The following year an anthology consisting of 18 poets, *Time X*, was published in Moscow in 1989, while Part II of the *White Square* collection came out in 1992 and included work by Arkady Turin and Karen Dzhangirov.

In the United States, however, Burich and Kupriyanov are not well known. Their work appeared in an anthology of Russian 20th century poetry, edited by Albert C. Todd et al. and published by Doubleday in 1993. They are represented in the book by a few short pieces from which it is difficult to ascertain the nature of their work and assess their contribution to prosody. Full course of the development of free verse from the mid-1950s and 1960s until today is yet to be fully evaluated by both Russian and American literary scholars and critics. This collection will give the readers a wider view of the creative work accomplished by Russian poets during the second half of the 20th century.

Samples of poems from the West end of the Slavic belt include poems in my translation by poets whose names I referred to earlier and who embraced free verse, making a contribution to its development in Croatia. The same is true for poets from Russia. In this collection are samples by early Russian free verse poets, among them Aigi, Mets, and Alekseev, as well as some younger representatives. But the most poems included here are by Vladimir Burich and Vyacheslav Kupriyanov. In making these selections I chose the poems that spoke to me and/or were looking for a translator; thus, they were transformed into another tongue. In addition to the poems, I am also including Mr. Kupriyanov's tribute to Vladimir Burich at the 75th Anniversary of the poet's birth, as well as "Reflections on Free Verse" by Arvo Mets. As far as jazz in Russia is concerned, there are a number of publications on the topic available, and, more recently, a detailed account of Valentin Parnakh's contributions and Dmitri Shostakovich's work by Lyubov Ginzburg which appeared recently in the *Journal of Russian-American Studies*.

I was introduced to Mr. Kupriyanov's poetry in the Croatian journal *Forum*, Nos. 10-12, 2002. The poems reminded me of work I was doing on Croatian poets, and I decided to try translating from Croatian. A colleague was able to bring me a copy of *Better Times* from Russia, so I could read the poems in their original Russian. In addition, I contacted Mr. Kupriyanov to obtain his permission to translate. My translations were published in several literary journals in the United States and abroad.

With the support from the university, I was able to invite Mr. Kupriyanov to our campus for a bilingual reading in 2008, and, a couple of years later, I took a colleague and poet from Kalamazoo College, Conrad Hilberry, to St. Petersburg for a bilingual reading by these two poets. At that time Mr. Hilberry was already acquainted with Mr. Kupriyanov's work, having read most of my translations in English and offered some suggestions. We all had a successful experience in this American-Russian exchange. However, it is unfortunate that I was unable to finish this project while Conrad Hilberry was still alive. I decided, therefore, to dedicate the book in his memory.

WEST SLAVIC BELT

SELECTED FROM EARLY TO MID-20TH CENTURY WORKS

JANKO POLIĆ KAMOV (1886-1910)

ANTUN BRANKO ŠIMIĆ (1898-1925)

AUGUSTIN UJEVIĆ (1891-1955)

DRAGUTIN TADIJANOVIĆ (1905-2007)

DRAGO IVANIŠEVIĆ (1907-1981)

JURE KAŠTELAN (1919-1990)

VESNA PARUN (1922-2010)

SLAVKO MIHALIĆ (1928-2007)

Janko Polić Kamov

Prelude

I will ravish you white paper, innocent paper;
vast is my passion and you'll barely bear it;
you dodge my fury and are pale with fright;
a kiss on your paleness – my kisses are black.

There is no law above you and laws are dead for me;
I escape them and my flight is swift;
I come from where they crawl with bowed heads,
where dogs praise orgies and licking is their lechery.

You dodge me, frightened hind, and tremble of first shame;
innocence is enticing and madness is its echo;
I am frenzied, O paper, and my temper blazes in my eye.

People are devoted and their tails are between their legs;
there is no truth in their eyes and dragging is their pace;
sniffing is their work and their pay is high;
there is no place for me among them and punitive is my word;
I swallow my thoughts and shame will smother me.

Stop, my love, and listen to my pain;
you take people's word – an ass has not yet understood a human;
oxen pull plows and slavery brings them hay;
a horse carries a boyar and its coat is shining;
swine eat well and their meat is savory:
slim and sharp are laws and stalls are full of oats.
Don't dodge me, kissed maiden, there is no woman for me;
they don't give of themselves to nervous kisses and stiff skin;
O I have no gold, nor is there a diploma without it.

I love you, paper, and my love is warm;
warm like my blood and frenzied like my temper.
Give yourself to me forever – black are my kisses;
black are my kisses, and red blood is in them.

ANTUN BRANKO ŠIMIĆ

My Transformations

One's self I sing when out of the abysmal and tortuous night
I bring up a pale soft face before the crystal morning
and gazing swim across the fields meadows and waters

I sing myself who numerous times a day dies
and numerous times resurrects

O Lord, let me tired of vicissitudes
be transformed into your bright unchangeable and eternal star
that will shine in the night from the far distant sky
at the dark anguish of tormented souls

Return

You don't even sense
my return and my proximity

At night when the quiet moonlight murmurs in your ear
know:
it's not the moonlight circling your house
It is I who wander the blue paths of your garden

When walking the street in the dull midday light
you pause
frightened by a cry of a strange bird
know:
that's my heart's scream from the nearby shores

And when at twilight you see a dark shadow moving
from the other side of the dark silent water
know:
I am walking upright and solemn
as if next to you

Poets

Poets are a wonder in the world

They walk the earth and their eyes
large and silent grow next to objects

Lending an ear
to the silence that surrounds and torments them
poets are eternal sparkles in the world

God Discovered

Don't seek God in thought; in emptiness
in which thought, dark shadow, disappears
God is by you, always near
in things around you, in sound and distress

God is always nearest of all to you
You touch him with your hand, look at him in the sky
God smiles at you from another's face
and frightens you of each thing: there's no secret

Don't spread thought into empty distance
God is by you. Open all the senses:

Light pours upon you from the summer sky

God around you shines flutters smells and rustles

A Warning

Watch out
you don't walk short
under the stars!

Let
the soft light of the stars
pass all over you!

That you regret nothing
when your last glances will
part with the stars!

In the end
instead into ashes
pass complete into the stars!

Death and I

Death is not outside of me. It is in me
from the very beginning: it grows with me
in every moment

        One day
I stop

   and it continues to grow
in me until it outgrows all of me
and arrives at my edge. My ending
is its real beginning:

                when it continues to rule alone

AUGUSTIN (TIN) UJEVIĆ

Everyday Lament

How hard it is to be so weak,
how hard it is to be alone,
and to be old, yet be so young!

And be weak, and be so helpless,
alone without anyone anywhere,
and be restless, and be hopeless.

And to be walking in the streets,
and be walked over in the mud,
without a star's shine in the sky.

Without the fated star shining
that sparkled above the cradle
with all the rainbows and the tricks.

O God, God, you must remember
all the radiant promises
that you had bestowed upon me.

O God, God, you must remember
all the love and the victory
and the laurel and all the gifts.

And know your Son is traveling
the valley of sorrowful world
over the thorns and over rocks,

from cruelty to hatefulness,
and his legs are very bloody,
and his heart is deeply wounded.

And his bones are very tired,
and his soul is so very sad,
and he's alone and abandoned.

He has no sister or brother,
he has no father or mother,
and he has no sweetheart or friend.

And he has no one anywhere
to the very pin of the thorn
in the heart and flames in his hands.

And all alone he now travels
under the very clear closed sky,
in front of the dark open sea,

and to whom is he to complain?
There's no one to listen to him,
neither the brothers who wander.

O God, your word scarred me deeply
and it's tight for it in the throat,
and it is wanting to cry out.

That utterance is a pyre
and I am obliged to shout it,
or my post will burst out in flames.

Let me be the fire in the hills,
let me be the breath of fire,
if not a cry from the rooftops!

O God, let it finally end
this melancholy wandering
under the sky that does not hear.

For I need a powerful word,
because I need a true answer,
and a real love, or holy death.

Bitter is the wreath of warm wood,
dark is the chalice of poison,
I cry glowing St. Elijah's.

Because it is hard to be weak,
and it is hard to be alone
(if only I could be stronger,

if only I could be dearer),
but it is so hard, the hardest
to be even old, yet so young!

Dragutin Tadijanović

To the One I Anticipate

Are the two of us
Far from each other?
O, if I could know
If there is blue longing
Between the two of us?…
You are a small girl
And you have black eyes,
Two black flames,
And I am perhaps your
Modest dear poet,
Who would like to sing to you
Happy songs from the heart, without rhyme;
But neither do I know where you are
Nor what is your name!

Ad Honorem et Gloriam
to Giacomo Leopardi's shadow

Unnoticed you entered my young heart
Which long ago then could not even
Fathom that the two of us, Giacomo,
Will secretly be friends for a whole century
And that I, perhaps, will be destined
At the end of my life's journey
To arrive at your steep hillside,
Listening to the murmur of the wind in the treetops,
And from the very same spot where you stood
Converse with infinity and eternity
And greet your shadow, forever alive.

Three Trees

Three trees in the field
Are always waiting for someone.

If the sun is shining, they say:
Stop by in the coolness of the shade.
And when the heart is heavy, they rustle:
Cry it all out under the leaves

And no one will ever know
About your tears, your sadness, your grief.
Only the dark earth will hear it
And these three trees in the field.

Drago Ivanišević

Dancer

She coils around me her feathery body
and wags her tail in the air
with animated hand she plays with her hair
barefooted
(I touch snow, fire, light ribbon)
she extinguishes my sight
a tide of passion chokes me in the dark
in fertile darkness a whirlwind of senses—
fireworks flash, fountains flow
an intoxicating torrent of sound
rises
it bathes my breath
it sets reason on fire
it's a radiant murderer of desire

Croatia

to Veco Holjevac

Neither the hills are,
nor the valleys, nor the rivers, nor the sea,
nor the clouds are,
nor rain, nor snow is
my Croatia…
Because Croatia is not earth, stone, water.
Croatia is the word I learned from my mother
and that in a word much deeper than the word
and that deeper ties me to Croatia,
to Croatia of the Croats,
to their sufferings,
to their laughter and hope,
it ties me to the people,
so I as a Croat am a brother to all the people.
And wherever I go, Croatia is with me!

Ars Poetica I

Because all the dead
who hunger
for life
in this land
are rotting
you must not be silent
you must not be silent listen
I am speaking to you
who are looking into the night
you who nowhere
see the stars I am speaking
to you
silent you must not be
you cannot be silent in this
night in this
night without the stars because
the dead forbid
silence because the horrible silence
of the dead loosens the tongue
and you speak
you speak into the night because
silent you cannot be
silent you must not be
in the night in this
night without the stars
your cry penetrates
the darkness in the darkness is an echo
an echo of all the dead
all the dead who hunger
for life in this

in this
land
are rotting
silent you must not be
you must not be silent
you cannot you must not

Silence

A fawn

JURE KAŠTELAN

Poplars

According to a grade school assignment

In my village there are many poplars.
They grow along streams and rivers,
in water they bend like eels.

My village is beautiful, because it has poplars.
Poplars grow high into the sky.
My mother calls me, my mother loves me:
O poplar, here is some water, my poplar.

Most poplars grow in my village
birds nest in them
clouds entangle in them
and the stars through them glide.

Stone's Lament

Return me into large mass, into cliffs, into mountain ranges.
Into the laws of eternity, my virginity.
Throw me into the seas, into oceans, turn me to thunders,
Rulers of the earth, give me peace and sleep.
Don't let your armies pound with their hoofs.
Don't let the tears flow.
Pull me out of sidewalks and streets, from thresholds of prisons
    and cathedrals.
Let the lightning and storms strike me. And let the stars crown me.
        And you, the hand that lifts a chisel,
        don't give me life of a human.
Give me neither a heart nor reason nor eyes that see.
Return me to marble seas, to dreams and fog.
Rulers of the earth, give me peace and sleep.
        And you, the hand that lifts a chisel, don't awaken me.
        Don't give me eyes that see evil.

Lullaby of Time

Don't forget
that under the stars nothing dies.

You who kill,
a corpse is stronger in its death.

You who love,
know fragrant swallows and chirping roses.

Don't forget
that under the stars you live only once.

You know fragrant swallows and chirping roses,
you who love.

Don't forget
that under the stars you die only once.

A corpse is stronger in its death,
you who kill.

Don't forget
that under the stars nothing dies.

A Fortress that Does Not Surrender

I am a fortress with a solitary flag of a heart.
Invisible walls built from wounds.
I resist invasions
with a lullaby.
Transformed into armor of a dream.
On all towers patrol, and at the shore hidden
boats of reed and tamarisk.
Anemometers watch distant iron armies sharpen arrows,
oil grease their thighs and biceps and rear up on evil horses
from tin-mines and fire.
The bridges are up and an irresistible torrent
prevents access.
And at dawn the moon disappears and serene sun appears.
I am a fortress with a solitary flag of a heart.
A fortress that does not surrender.
The dead freed of their senses do not surrender.
Lightning in fast flight does not surrender.
The living with eyes of jewels do not surrender.
Strongholds surrender, but not those of dreams.
They give of themselves and by themselves resist.
I am a fortress with a solitary flag of a heart.

Votive Light

From antiquity to antiquity
From distances to distances
    it smolders
    burns
    flickers
for a horse in the hills for a boat at high seas
for shadows of the dead for pupils of the living
    holy
    olive
    oil

VESNA PARUN

I Was a Boy

The evening, having turned off
the candles, hid me in the moonlight.
In the azure forest through the trees
I thoughtfully dreamt all night.

I was a grape from a red cluster
in the teeth amidst kisses
a fox that ran out of a snare
a boy, who throws shouts with a sling;

and a bite of a song in the middle of a forehead
a brindled cat in a play basket.
What haven't I been, what haven't I dared,
a mirror of a fish in the pupil of an otter!

A Child and a Meadow

Only a child clearly hears in the moss
the flutter of fast spring, the twitter in the feathers of the kingfisher.
It wanders after brooks, kisses juniper trees in the sun
while the eyes assume the color of the nearby hill.

The child weaves the beauty of the morning with a smile
without paying attention to the permanence of some sound
spread by chance, in the wind.

Children are echoes of extinct things.
Bare and pure as a fish pond, they see themselves
in the face of the meadow, in the snare of the spider.

Mother of Mankind

It would have been better had you given birth to black winter,
   mother dear, than to me.
Had you given birth to a bear in a burrow, a snake on a log.
And had you kissed a stone, rather than my face,
it would have been better had I been nursed by the udder of a
   beast, than by a woman.

And had you given birth to a bird, mother dear, you would be
   a mother.
You would be happy, you would warm the bird under your wing.
If you had given birth to a tree, the tree would come to life in
   the spring,
the lime tree would blossom, from your song the reed would turn
   green.

By your feet a lamb would rest, had you been a mother to a lamb.
If you babble and cry, the kind beast would understand you.
This way, you stand alone and alone you share your stillness with
   the graves;
it is bitter to be a man, as long as man takes a knife for a friend.

A Coral Returned to the Sea

I am returning this scarlet hoop of sun, this star of the earth in the
    mirror of the sea,
embodied sight of life which cannot be uprooted, which grows
in the colony of live marine roots and large, immobile fish.
I am returning what I took at the beginning to decorate myself like
    a plant for the celebration of people and spring
before the morning icon of light and winds from afar.
I am returning the seed of life, this red branchlike flower
that is neither stone nor shell nor salt nor vine nor seed
but lives and grows and can become a mountain in the center of
    the ocean.
I am returning my youth and my death and everything that a tree
    made from morning to night.
I am returning sails to the high seas and birds to the land,
creeks to clover, nests to chests of light in the east,
tenderness to the bitter and confused, courage to those assembled
    for departure,
solitude to the stray moon, sadness to the herds from the mountain
    dawn.
I am returning a cradle to the sea, I am separating the fire into two
    flint stones
and I am continuing to tread down untrodden roads of my life
which is taken over by the march of the stars and the abundance
    of silence.

Epilogue

I shall never be
a prickly grass
and black robbers
will not tread upon me.
Everything I once
gave to this sky
time will return to me
with each of its
birds.
I shall never be
a trampled grass
and I will rustle clearly
so the children
understand me.
Who passes by me
will be happy.
And the bell, the old sinner,
will cease to toll.

SLAVKO MIHALIĆ

Otherwise Everything Would Be Meaningless

They say: people begin to die in the cradle
It seems to me – they rise from the dead
Then live all the more
Eyes open in all colors
Hands then necks and other parts of the body begin to work
In the end time comes for things we call
    the interior
Actually no one has seen them
That doesn't mean they're not there – they hide cleverly
    from the murderers
Life is that little something under the cover of soap bubbles
Go ahead, say nothing
If you blow at it
You'll be a little less wrong
But the dead man will return again
Otherwise everything would be meaningless

It Is, It Is Time

Perhaps it is time
to keep love secret.
It needs to be hidden
in the basement of some deserted
house.
Cut out of flesh,
clothed in beggarly rags.
Close its mouth,
seal its eyes.
Knock it off a cliff,
burn, and its dust
spread to all four
sides.

It is, it is time
when poetry also is a crime.

Farewell to Oneself

Now is the moment for each of us
to go our separate ways: you, legs, follow the footsteps
of which you dream as soon as I lie down;
hands wherever – the left, clumsy, into the parts
of the imagination, the right with the armies; the fingers and toes,
all twenty of them, will go perhaps to some other world;
this one, they think, they've destroyed enough;
after them the ribs, the workers, wounded;
the liver, it's known, will go into the nearest pub (where
the kidneys, the stomach, and the bladder are lapping it up);
the heart will go to the barricade, but without blood,
whispering, so much allotted for love fights;
the lungs between the clouds, the brain into the very sun;
and I will remain alone with this ugly
tongue, created for distinction but it continuously
babbled, got me into the worst situations.
Come on now, tongue, show me what you can do,
now when I am left without anything: fill up the basement,
    the attic, the pantry.

Coffee Cantata

Please, coffee, remain
only what you are: morning's first tenderness.
For the incomparability of your color
and the nobility of the poison with which you revive me,
henceforth do not mention your honorable
origin, hardships on your path to my lips,
secret intentions. As it is, everything that reason
could grasp pales before the equilibrium
which, in one gulp, you establish
in my room. Everything is moving around a single
center, and all is the center, glistening, resounding,
unyielding. Never is time so
in tune with my will as when you, little dark
animal, scrape over the edge
of my entrails. Then, in my own way of hearing,
I conduct the murmur of the treetops under
the windows. But the treetops are no longer there,
and that is what I would not want to lose with continuous
repetition of history, published causes;
the ability to be where one is not,
complete control of things without meaning. With coffee
at our lips we age for all the folly of the world
and feel how sweetly roots burn.

A Whirl

The mind comes late. It's delayed by infinite
music, wants to sing in Monteverdi
madrigals, play the harpsichord in Bach's
Well-Tempered Clavier. Drink a jug of
Opolo in a garden restaurant. Embrace
love across all seas and mountain
ranges, never to arrive at the end.

The body on the contrary rushes, with a steel cable
ties the beginning and the end. From weakness falls
onto its emaciated palm which draws for it a picture
of destiny. It forgets. Howls at others
without seeing it walks with them. Buries a pernicious
thought in a secret place for which it then
frantically looks praying not to find it.

The soul at departure watches all this
from the fence. Heavenly whirl is already pulling it.
It asks itself what out of everything can it take:
love which is counterbalance among things,
a pernicious thought which straightens its bones,
a deed which unites the fools.
And it doesn't suspect the doors above are locked.

EAST SLAVIC BELT

SELECTED FROM EARLY 20TH THROUGH 21ST CENTURY

GENNADY ALEKSEEV (1932-1987)

GENNADY AIGI (1934-2006)

ARVO METS (1937-1997)

EUGENE BRAYCHUK (b. 1948)

DMITRY GRIGORIEV (b. 1960)

ARSEN MIRZAEV (b. 1960)

VLADIMIR BURICH (1932-1994)

VYACHESLAV KUPRIYANOV (b. 1939)

Gennady Alekseev

Variations on the Theme of Existentialism

1. Freedom from the Absurd
   I draw from the absurd ... my freedom
                              —Camus

I draw from the absurd
Two little monkeys
They are all over the room
They jump on the chairs
They swing from the chandelier
And hurl at me different items:
Heavy bronze candleholders
Pounds of cast iron dumbbells
And huge bullions of pure gold
Where did they find all this?

I am not drawing freedom from the absurd
I will show you what I draw

Between

I remain between the beginning and the end
—KARL JASPERS

How sad
I still remain
Between the beginning and the end
It is bad for me here
In the middle

It was good until the beginning
Oh how wonderful it was until the beginning!
Until the beginning I was simply in a state of bliss

But sadly
It began

I hope it will not be bad
After the end

My Gifts to Pieter Bruegel

With his peasants
I danced at a wedding
Spirited enough

With his hunters
I hunted hares
Quite successfully
In his hell
The devils tortured me
And quite zealously
And in one of his blind men
I found myself
In that
fourth one
With helplessly opened mouth

Later
I matured
(that happens)
Matured and saw everything
And climbed a road amidst a field
And grass on the side roads
And I saw the blind strolling on the roads
and I despaired—
There were too many
blind

May 28, 1981

And One More Hamlet

A thousand times I asked myself:
To be or not to be? And answering a thousand times
I shrugged my shoulders.
Then I began to ask
Everyone else:
To be or not to be?
To be or not to be?
To be or not to be?
And answering all shrugged their shoulders.
Then I got angry
Caught a seven-year-old boy in the yard
Grabbed him by the ear
And began to shout:
Stinker Speak
To be or not to be?
The boy began to cry
And avoided answering.
In sorrow I got drunk
Like a pig.
Staggering
I was going down Nevsky
Reading neon signs.
They were all the same.
Above a store was a sign:
TO BE OR NOT TO BE?
At the entrance to a movie theater:
TO BE OR NOT TO BE?
In a window of a beauty shop:
TO BE OR NOT TO BE?
On top of a beer bar:

TO BE OR NOT TO BE?
In a streetcar I couldn't restrain myself
And asked the conductress:
Well, for all that—
To be or not to be?
Good heavens!
Replied the conductress,
But what's the difference!

Trap

My sorrow is my trap
—KIERKEGAARD

Welcome to
My unhappy trap!
I alone will lower the drawbridge
And lift up to the tower
The flag of endless sorrow—
By the light of smoky torches
We enter into a gloomy vaulted hall
And give ourselves to the dark
Motionless trapeze

Who among us is most unhappy
I ask suddenly
At the peak of the feast

And a chorus of voices replies:
I am!

October 23, 1979

The Wall of Misfortune

*The wall upon which we come
and where we suffer misfortune*

—KARL JASPERS

Oh, yes
The wall
High
Thick
Long
Like the Great Wall of China

I dragged a ladder
Climbed up to the top
Looked at
What's beyond the wall
And was struck
Oh, no
There is no purpose to that wall
We suffer an absolute misfortune!

Variations on the Theme of Humanity

The weather is rotten
the mood nasty
disposition disgusting
and humanity is in trouble
it wandered off
devil knows where

the lamp burned out
the glass broke
the boots got holes in them
and insignificant humanity
poor thing lost its way
in broad daylight

the weather will change
the mood will improve
the attitude will get better
but what will happen
to humanity?

save it
risking one's life
or turn away
indifferently?
or laugh in its face
and say:
well deserved?
(endless troubles with that humanity!
eternal confusion!)

guess it has to be saved
but how?

who knows
how to save humanity?
hey!
who knows
how to save humanity?
he-he-hey!
who knows
how to save our unhappy humanity?
whoever
knows how to save our beautiful humanity
please let me know about it
by phone

my number is: 217-30-47

September 23, 1981

Splinter

I am a small
splinter
hidden under the dust
a splinter
of something big
of something former
of something lost

a splinter of ancient architecture
mutilated by the barbarians?
a splinter of Gothic stained-glass windows
broken by little boys?
a splinter of a colossal statue
lost during an earthquake?
a splinter of an enormous meteorite
that burst on the surface of the earth?

pick me up
wipe off the dust
examine me
rotate in your hands
and tell me
whose splinter am I

GENNADY AIGI

Road

When no one loves us
we begin
to love our mothers

When no one writes to us
we recall
old friends
and utter words only because
silence is unbearable
and movements dangerous

In the end – in neglected parks
we cry listening to sad trumpets
in sad orchestras

And Those Who

And those who from the very moment
they first saw God's world
began to differentiate
black from white
delighted they hurried to inform
here – this is white

Rustling of the Birches
to V. Korsunsky

and I am also rustling:
"and it may be God..."—

whispering in the birches:
"died..."—

and we
disintegration that continues?—

and why
not?—

solitary and deserted ashes disperse...

(whispering birches...
we all in the world rustle...)—

and again
will Rise?..—

even not painfully:

as forever...

a stir – as about that!..—

.... –

(like abandoned – autumn stir)

1975

Rain

it drizzles and subsides
as if playing with itself "chance"

(like a valid endowment
only for pitiable sketches)

as if it "exists" "lives"
(in a circle – like **I** – superfluous)

Clearer than Sense

O
Transparence! one day
Enter and Expand yourself

with a poem

1982

Without a Title

(from the last notes)

Yes, – even a bird dies
together with its song,—
and what a song and what a bird!—
don't feel sorry for yourself, – the song is on the Earth—

May 2, 2005, Rodos

ARVO METS

from **IN AUTUMN FORESTS** (1992-1996)

The Soul

The soul
is so quiet
in autumn forests.

It hears
its voice,
suppressed for ages.

A Poet Stands in Line for Vermicelli

A poet stands in line for vermicelli.
Here are his female admirers.
The poet is a little ashamed.
He stood on the stage,
like a small prince,
who never eats.

Houses, Trams

Houses, trams.
Stores, dishes.
I walk among them,
like a Martian
among monuments
of an unknown civilization,
erected carelessly
for basic needs.
…And somewhere inside
in quiet corners are
crystals of music.

I Am the Spirit of Contemplation

I am the spirit of contemplation.
Somewhere on earth
walks the spirit of action
and does everything
without me.
We are two big spirits
sad in our incompleteness.
In a divided world
many things
seek one another.

Where to Find

Where to find
enough happiness
for all the people,
in the city squares?

In the eyes
of each one
the soul struggles
like a butterfly
between windowpanes.

I Am in Love

I am in love
with the beauty
of simple things,
which quietly burn,
like ash berry
in an autumn garden.
In youth
we race
past them.
And only later
find our
real friends.

While Alive

While alive
he never kept airs,
my modest
unnoticed father,
as lying down in his grave.
Bent, he
displays
an eagle's profile
similar to those
they usually
engrave on coins.

In Memory of Erni

(excerpt)

Work.
Now and then smile.
Get married and bear children.
Send them, like letters, into the future.
And transform again into the earth.
Concealed in life is some stubborn sense,
I also seek.

Engines

Engines,
collected by us,
were all
alike.

It's hard to distinguish
the work of a criminal
from the work
of a poet.

Far

Far,
as if looking through old binoculars,
lives my mother
in a wooden house.
In the evening she returns
to a cold room,
having fumbled out of habit
through her empty mailbox.

A Homeless Dog

A homeless dog
adapts its walk
by pretending
as if it's going
on an invisible leash.

A person turns away
and it gradually
stays behind.

Poplar Fluff

Poplar fluff
flies through the window
of a respected establishment.
There is some kind of tenderness
in its flight,
and that is dangerous.
A typist could forget
herself,
recollect youth,
stop typing.
And even an important fellow
could suddenly
become sad
like a little boy.

Young Girls' Faces

Young girls'
faces resemble
the sky,
the wind,
the clouds.
Then they become
faithful wives,
whose faces resemble
homes,
furniture,
shopping bags.

But their daughters'
faces again resemble
the sky, the wind
and streams of spring.

What Does One Call

What does one call
these white berries
in Russian,
I never found out.

And what are they
in Estonian –
I forgot...

Neither Do I Know

Neither do I know,
how to me,
befell the fate
of a Russian poet.

...with all its consequences.

My Estonia

My Estonia,
little,
beyond wind-fallen trees,
beyond overflowing rivers.

Just breaks off
and flows out
into distance.

Father

Father
was sparing
on feelings,
but when he worked,
I saw it myself —
silent goodness
in his hands
transformed
into sublime kindness.

October

Leaves lie,
like injured birds,
small paws upward.

On Such Dark Evenings

On such dark evenings
one can get light
only from books.

A Man with a Violin

A man
with a violin
entered a grocery store.
A nagging compassion
suddenly arose in him—
he looked so ridiculous
among counters
and in the crowd.

… And I
with my
invisible violin?

A Birch Leaf

A birch leaf
tore away from the tree.
And slowly flies into eternity.

EUGENE BRAYCHUK

Jazz

Look how tastefully the saxophonist
kisses the bill
of his silver cygnet!
And how strained are the piano arrangements,
as if playing with a magnificent structure
of powerful consonances!
In their gentle and passionate biceps
the melody twists and moans,
decreases and rises,
transforming into an infinite voice!

O!
This improvisation
is doing what it wants with the melody!

And it tolerates it.

This Penetrating, Almost X-ray Music

This penetrating, almost X-ray music
lights up all the little bones –
each bright from delight.

Yes. While listening to favorite music,
as if I were created by the wands,
beaming from the surge of magic!

Distant, Silent Words and Phrases

Distant, silent words and phrases –
almost breaths in sound of the epoch
in the very alveolus of time,
which in drops drip down the shaft of the soul,
filling it with purity and chime.
But from that ringing scatter
sleeping in us forefathers
of unresolved questions.
And they create commotion
from which it is hard to breathe...

DMITRY GRIGORIEV

Elections

I elect the birds,
flying off somewhere unknown,
stones fall, the bulletin board whitens,
and I stand next to the open door,
rooms full of sand,
cats jump higher and higher,
dogs spin their tails like helicopters,
delegates carry their mandates,
deputies take their places,
and I cast my vote
for the heavenly birds.

War

The country weaves a wreath,
the thorns pierce the fingers,
and the red fingers flow.
Be silent: "Tulips, poppies,
they grow upon these hills…"
Will words really stop the blood?

And we stand, stand the ground,
above us the dogs urinate
standard-bearers graze the day…
I saw the black wagons,
there the word LAD
sounds like LEAD.

What's in the Backpack

—What's in the backpack?—
they ask at customs.

—There's some earth,
fake mushrooms,
empty space
not sacred,
and this, the road back.

—That's too much,
they say.
—Pour out the earth,
plant the mushrooms,
put yourself in the empty space.
The road back—
take it with you—
it's of no interest to us.

I cross the border
already without strength to stop.

ARSEN MIRZAEV

She Turned Around Finally

She turned around finally
disembarked
dissolving
into the morning crowd

and the train continued

for some reason
in front of me
persistently stood
almond-shaped
sad eyes
of deer
in a drawing by Pirosmani…

At Dawn

a condition
when you're half asleep
and half awake
when it's still unknown
who you are—
a man or a woman

half blissful morning
half morning-unisex

Silences

To Gennady Aigi

one

words flow
like a river
the soul is silent

another one

words
of the last drop will stop short
and fall
it begins to speak

the other

a different soul
will live
silently
grand
in a river
in the last
drop

Soc-Intellect-And-I (СОЦИУМИЯ)

deep down I am an artist
I perform
every second, every moment
in very different
auditoriums

each time
the reaction
is immediate:
powerful
one hand
applause

My Book Is Coming Out

My book is coming out
but I remain
dragging
as before
a miserable existence
in s o m e o n e e l s e 's
space

To a Poet

1.

speed up your demise
let the people
evaluate you

speed up your demise
let the people
pity you

speed up your demise
give us
a cause...

2.

speed up your demise
don't detain
clever and honest people

speed up your demise
sculptors linger
in their studios

speed up your demise
well, now –
we're waiting – we can't wait

speed up your demise
all the same
there's nothing to gain

speed up your demise
let's sit awhile,
feel sad, smoke some

speed up your demise
you'll drink with us
on the house

3.

speed up your demise
we guarantee you
eternal glory

speed up your demise
we offer lodging
free of charge

speed up your demise
ladies' man, swindler,
plagiarist, scum

speed up your demise
cur, riff-raff,
scribbler

speed up your demise
time has expired,
the ink has dried up

speed up your demise
February is a good time
to die

VLADIMIR BURICH

from **WHITE SQUARE** (1988)

What Do I Expect

What do I expect of tomorrow's day?
Newspapers

As I Grow Old

As I grow old
I will walk short of breath
from asthma
unbuttoned
in any kind of weather
with a secret hope
that someone will notice
my medal
for the defense
of human
dignity

So Why Am I Afraid to Die

So why am I afraid to die
if I lie down to sleep with a prayer
that everyone outlives me

The Sun Replaces the Moon

The Sun replaces the Moon
The Sun is replaced by the Moon

One Sun
One Moon

Only pure chance
is preventing the development
of human imagination

Why Embrace

why embrace
if you can't smother ·

why kiss
if you can't swallow

why take
if you can't take it with you
forever
there
to the heavenly garden

About One Hundred People in this World Know Me

About one hundred people in this world know me
How boring will be their topic of conversation

I'm Going for Water

I'm going for water
as chamomile blossoms brush against
the bottom of my bucket

Tear Off Me the Binding of Vision

Tear off me the binding of vision
Strike off my arms the chains of what was done

O that first lake
reflecting the first cloud

City Rules

On leaving, I shut off the light.
I cross the street at the crossings.
First I look to the left, cross to the middle, look to the right.
I watch for the cars.
I watch for autumn.
I don't smoke.
I don't quarrel.
I don't walk on lawns.
I eat washed fruit; I drink boiled water.
I drink Champagne and natural juices.
After eating I wash my hands.
Before bedtime I brush the teeth.
I don't read in the dark or lying down.
And so I lived to the age of twenty-six.
And then what?
Save my money in a savings account?

Motto

A human
all possible variants of white
from red to blue

A human
countless variants of soft
from solid to liquid

A human
endless variants of good
from force to self-sacrifice

All occurrences and objects named by the outcry of the throat
length-size parts of the body became the first scale of the universe

Modus Vivendi

I reside
in a cube of a room
in a sphere of a balloon
in a pyramid of a rocket

I create
and love
these forms

I die
at each attempt
of the geometrizing
of my
body

Duty to Kill

Duty to kill
Duty to resist

A being with a midlife at sixty
kills
a being with a midlife at sixty

This sky is without principles like a prostitute
This house this earth are without principles like a prostitute

O anguish
despair
and chill
of a being
transforming itself into earth

Hatred Is Destructive

Hatred is destructive
love needs forms

How difficult it is to create
at the table
of a destroyed planet

Yes, Yes, Peace

Yes
yes
peace

but who will answer
for the fact that smashed walnuts seem to me skulls
for the fact that as before I have not decided
to spread butter on bread
for the fact that pawnshops hair salons baths railway stations
smell of mass killings

Yes
yes
peace

but who will answer for these lifelong visions

A Nation

A nation
feels itself
with sculptors' hands

Stupefied
it rises majestically
on the pedestals
of its
cities

It Is Possible

It is possible
the world from the start
was black-white

and the deaf-mute nature
with the help of colors
gave us some kind of signs

And we
mixed the alphabet of colors
having painted the earth
 the sky
 the waters

The secret remains undisclosed

Is It Possible?

Is it possible to tell a flower it is ugly?

I Looked at Her

I looked at her
didn't see her

I saw the sun spring from the sea

a palm branch floating on waves

the seashore

I looked at her
didn't see her

I saw mother's gown on the clothesline

myself bathing in a washtub

I saw

Suddenly disintegrated

head
torso
hands
feet

If Your Heart Were On the Outside

If your heart were on the outside
separate
somewhere near the collarbone
a lot would be clear

Unseen
it overgrows
with the legend of vessels

A Spade

A spade
is the lightning conductor of my despair

Only the earth knows
its exertion
and strength

Time X

In a suit and mask
with a dosimeter before me
I am going
to interview the earth

tell me
what happened
with what did they poison you

fatally ill
what is your last wish

you didn't recognize me
I've come to resemble vermin

I didn't recognize you
you are covered
with ulcers
of moon craters

Insomnia

I am listening
to the heartbeat of the pillow

I see
a mirror
a soundless echo

I think
about the fish
of prehistoric oceans

with an idea of humans
in the womb

Dream (1)

A huge
creature
from ocean to ocean
lies
eats
bread with metal

and something else

why doesn't it let the bread dry
and the metal rust

Home

Home
a cocoon
over which
winds the thread
of my life

cut
the unnecessary loops
leading to the forest
onto the sandy beach

some may stumble over them
going to the village store
for bread

I Glanced at My Window at Night

I glanced at my window at night

And saw
I was not there

And understood
I may not be

Death In the Country

Death in the country
is clearer
and more candid

All know
into what soil they buried him
what land he left behind

The wife
digging potatoes
cuts with the spade the face of her deceased husband

So I Could Not Finish

So I could not finish
the golden loaf of the day

I looked at the watch
mid-seventies

one must go to sleep
extinguish the light
in the eyes

One may raise arms
in order to capitulate

in order to fly off

Triptych

1

Allow me to gather
the falling stars
in your yard

2

Crucifixion
is only a representation
of ancient torture

3

The birds are terrified
at how loudly we breathe

Deadaptation

Already I don't remember the names of the stars
This will not be of use to me

Already I don't remember the names of countries
This will not be of use to me

Already I don't remember the names of the cities
names of squares

This
will not be
of use to me

I'll try to remember your face
the price of bread
and the number of my apartment

On the Avenue

On the avenue
in fear hiding their faces with the newspaper
the retirees
sit
in anticipation of death

Old Christ and Judas play checkers
the robbers boast they too were crucified
Mary knits mittens for grandchildren

At her feet
the children
are building out of sand
the tower of Babel

We Are Talking With the Teacher

We are talking with the teacher on the steps of a temple
The steps come up to the crown of my head
I see enormous toes in sandals
grass
growing out of the stone's nostrils

And I don't understand
a word

We Are Walking

We are walking
over underground rivers
treasures
pressed by the skylines

I can count by heart
the order
of layers of black earth and clay
in its burial hole

I thought
eternity—
two thousand years of our era

it is
only
two meters
down deep
from the stem of wormwood

The Last Bird on My Branches

the last bird on my branches

the last ray on my bark

my trunk is bending
pouring out
the juice of love

Farther

Farther and
farther is
my university
shore

Wise books are getting wet with tears
and drown

Mom
why didn't you say
everything would be so

why did you teach me letters

Quieter is the singing of old Orpheuses
Rarer is the smell of rotten meat

And Still Another Generation

and still another generation
passed
by the platform
of youth
singing
waving flowers

around the corner
on freight cars
carefully setting down banners
hair
teeth

in the planned lane
receiving masks
for
the night carnival

Where Is My Body

where is my body
lacerated by thorns of the years?

where is my blood
remaining on thousands of hands?

where are my eyes
looking at me from other planets?

where am I?

Epitaph

Life is
a spark
struck by the stick
of the blind

And When the Sand Fell

and when the sand fell
on the watch of the lord god
he leveled it out
and made
a circus ring

The World

The world
collapsed
when it appeared
the inside walls of my destroyed school
were red

The world
collapsed
when I saw
the narrow street
which till then I considered endless
was cut off
by an anti-tank explosion

The world
collapsed
when in the frozen aquarium I saw
surprised eyes
of the fish

It collapsed
and returned into an abyss
which can be filled
neither by the bodies of beloved women
nor by poems

The World Is Being Filled

The world is being filled by
post-war people
post-war objects

I found among the letters
a piece of pre-war soap
I didn't know what to do
wash
or cry

Pre-war era—
a sunk Atlantis

And we
survived by a miracle

The Earth

The earth
heals itself
with grasses

it adds weeds
to unhealed
wounds
of the roads

Conceptions

I live
surrounded by
continuously changing conceptions of dwelling

I move
by means of
multiple conceptions of self-propelled organs

I watch a film
only the last 300 meters
correspond to the author's conceptions of 8 a.m. today

Creating my own conception of microcosm
I was almost crushed
by someone's geopolitical conception of the world

Careful!
This is
my life
one conception of immortality

Humanity

Humanity
an un-sunk vessel

Five billion
compartments
of hope

Ode to Maximalism

I want everything at once

I cannot condescend to the insignificant

And I feel
fixated forms of the bridge stuck in my throat
and my eyes lacerated by the fivehundredthirtythreemeter mast
of the television tower

And from the summit of my point of view slides a tear
bathing and distorting the panorama of the city

Theorem of Melancholy

On the tip of the elbow
is inscribed the circumference of the head

It is not necessary
to prove
anything

Little Box

Little box
of tooth
powder

you are amazingly clean
and chaste

No
I cannot…

Where is that empty toothpaste?

Your Head on the Pillow

Your head on the pillow
a frozen bird on the snow

What Was I Doing While You Were Growing Up?

Interesting
what was I doing
while you were growing up?

what was I doing?

it seems I was running after bread
no
I was laying a stone upon stone
or perhaps climbing the stairs
standing
dressing
looking around
giving change
missing the bus
sitting down to lunch
burying mother
eight years I was burying mother
running after bread
how strange
though we are close by
you were never able to catch up with me in that race
I cannot wait for you
I am only capable of rushing
you are beautiful
but what can I do with you
with you I can neither cry over the past
nor with hope look toward the future
of which
there is
less

We wave to each other with our hands
like swimmers
in aquariums
of departing trams

Migration

Every spring they aim for the south
to return for a time into amphibians

to change from place to place
a few pebbles

to submerge into the green water
with a taste of death

With the fall of temperature
they roam to the north
to deposit the eggs of remembrance

Armstrong

Black angel
announcing the end of the Harp

Prometheus
bound to the trumpet

Black and White

Black
seeks white
to kill in it the light
and turn it into grey
or stripe

A Butterfly

A butterfly
is an agreement about beauty
having equal power
on both wings

Café "Blue Bird"

The trumpeter left with bloody lips

The old man dozes over a wine glass

The girl
propping her hand on the elbow
holds a cigarette with two fingers:
"I believe"

Pure Coincidence

The Sun replaces the Moon
The Sun is replaced by the Moon

One Sun
One Moon

A pure coincidence
only delaying development
of human imagination

BREAKFAST

BREAKFAST
LUNCH
DINNER
BREAKFAST
LUNCH
DINNER

With pleasure I'll have a bite of the bait
enticing
tomorrow

In the Land of Violins

In the land of violins
Piano keys also sink

Ode to Friendship

We share with them homes
summer houses
dogs
garages
markets
clinics
cemeteries
daycare centers

Long live our friendship!
Our friendship is indestructible!

Contacts

We sit
smiling
with smiles of foolish lovers

How degrading not to understand another

We sit
smiling

We speak through a vacuum
      distance
      glass
      epoch

You begin to doubt whether a glass is a glass
              a lamp a lamp

Everything is anonymous

We sit
smiling

I am powerless to penetrate his microcosm
and noticed
I am beginning to study him as a biologist
            a commissar
            a hunter

I am at a concert of foreign words

I hurt

My head is packed with paper clips of Latin alphabet

STAGNATION

O the astonishment of my generation coming to life

CIRCLE
TRIANGLE
SQUARE

O joy O delight of my generation coming to life

SPHERE
PYRAMID
CUBE

O the anguish of my generation having come to life

ONEHUNDREDFIVEANGLED PYRAMID
ONEHUNDREDFIVE SPHERE
ONEHUNDREDSIXANGLED PYRAMID
ONEHUNDREDSIXPLANE SPHERE
ONEHUNDREDSEVENANGLED PYRAMID...

1963

Well How?

—Well how?—
he asked

when abandoned by secretaries
chairmen presidents bloodline princes
I was sitting on a park bench in the evening

What "how"?
What could I have answered him?

1964

Is It Possible I Will

Is it possible I will
all my life go like a chumak on highways
from a publisher to a journal
from a journal to a newspaper
where in each editor's armchair
sits its own Ahasu

Humanism

The bus goes not toward the people
The bus goes toward the bus stop

Everything Develops in a Spiral

Everything develops in a spiral
agreed the snail

hiding
still
deeper

Do Not Be Ashamed

Do not be ashamed to look where the crowd is looking
There may be a new automobile or perhaps a human being

October in Russia

October in Russia
is a critical time of the year

there is neither snow
to see a drop of blood

nor flowers
to decorate fresh graves

I Still Respect Those Who Are Older than I

Unscrupulously I still respect those who are older than I
Humiliatingly I compete with those of my own age
Pusillanimously I ignore those younger than I

When I will be as old as the earth
then

Escalation

I buy the paper
and hear the rustle of the leaves

I open the pages
and hear the crunch of the branches

in fern columns
I find the corpse
of my brother

Night

I am lying on my back
looking at the ceiling
with my ears filled with tears

Morning

I awoke
and in amazement understood
that I was leaving my body
without supervision
in care
of the stars
the grass
the pine trees
and the wind

Sleep

Sleep
a sweet drop of non-being

What are you like death?

The Face of a Girl Is a Meadow

The face of a girl is a meadow
the face of a maiden a garden
the face of a woman a home
home full of women's worries

Grey Little Bird

Grey little bird
with a yellow speck on your chest

let me kill you
so I can examine you

Transplantation

I came with a spade
and transplanted the roots
the eyes
the heart

I entangled everything
in the place of a kidney
grew a green ear

And Life Is Simple

And life is simple like an astronaut's breakfast

An Unfinished Home

An unfinished home
thoughts of summer
of children
of happiness

Finished home
thoughts of major repairs
heirs
death

Midlife

Midlife
thoughts at the summit

Everything is happening precisely and simply
as in an operating room
without the interception of light

They Bloom Out

They bloom out
they fall off
the petals of neckties
the skin of the suits
the peel of the shoes
and what remains is
the naked sense of my life
at first glance needed by no one
like the green
inedible
seeds of potatoes

Just As the Face Got Used to Shaving

Just as the face got used to shaving

It is time to die

Fame Is

Fame is
a prison of smiles
behind the walls of which
awaits
patient death

Life Is

Life is
a gradual removal
of masks

until the last one

of plaster

In Front of Me a Gigantic Basin of an Olympic Stadium

In front of me a gigantic basin of an Olympic stadium
filled with white and black beans...

And in my mind I just cannot divide my ashes
between my favorite countries and cities

Vyacheslav Kupriyanov

from **TIME X** (1989)

In a Former World

In a former
world
a prohibition was issued
preventing people to feed
on anything but
birds' milk.

And the obedient
died.
Only those in power
who introduced the ban
remained
for on the side they had meat.

And those who resisted the ban
were banished
into distant lands
condemned to bread and water.

A Song

In one
once former world
the Ones had a song
which was taken from them
by the Others.

And then the Ones composed
another song
and with it went
to the Others
and took from them their first song
and simultaneously the lives of the Others.

But now the Ones didn't know
what they liked better—
the song for which
they fought against the Others—
or the song
which led them to the Others

in a quandary
they disappeared from the face of the earth
the Ones after the Others
in one once
former world.

The World

The world sounds
as if all idiots
became musicians
their hard foreheads
lovingly
collide
and give rise to freedom
from the present

The world is watched
like a detective series
all await continuation
considering themselves heroes
and not victims
of idle curiosity:
daily mass suicide
in a whirlpool of television

This world
wants to be for any taste
the blood is already discolored
everything is tasteless

This world
smells of means of transportation
contraception

only the lack of means
inspires hope
for the future

Cosmic Events

Through the heavenly bodies
of women

in flight
to and from the universe
cosmic little
children
fly by

Some of them
remain
in order
to grow

A Person With a Knife

A person with a knife
Is not concerned
About what
Thoughts
Are ripening
In the bulb of an onion

Where by the way
There are
Tears

Everything Around Me and I Everywhere

Everything around me and I everywhere
the rain is one and a half kilometers from me
the sun some one and a half million
the moon almost four hundred thousand
slightly over four light years
and I in the vicinity of alpha center
ten steps and I will drown in the fog
ten minutes and the twilight will swallow me
only an hour and I am in a pine grove
lost among three pine trees
in an hour I am at the newspaper stand
and in the papers they write about the whole world
so small
as if one can talk about it in the newspapers

In Anticipation

In anticipation
of a fiery life
heroes
sleep courageously

in a matchbox

from **FORUM** (a Croatian literary journal; Nos. 10-12 2002)

I Am Swimming Deep Under Water

...I am swimming deep under water
with open eyes, around me
with increasing speed
narrows the orbit in which
sharks scurry about, soaking up water
that separates them from me, and I
cannot swallow in time
and feel: sharks
share me
among
themselves
I am drowning in my own blood
and scream as I am losing myself
in horror I awake and see:
there is not a drop of water
only I whole in cold sweat
above me a huge hot sun
around dry desert
it narrows around me
in growing yellow clumps
of fearful yellow lions
that rush toward me
leaving behind
emptiness in the expanse of the desert
but I am not terrified
having met the sharks
the lions seem to me

royal killers
deserving to kill
they throw themselves at me
in a single sandy jaw of the desert
they share me
among themselves
I suffocate in my own blood
I scream
holding on
to the possibility
of a cry
in horror I awake and see:
above me a cold city sky
with lost toys of the stars
and around me
almost inaudible
closes in an ominous chorus
of men and women, youth and maidens
elders and children
many of them with arms open
to embrace, capture and strike
their hands come down upon me
they close in around me
they share
me
among
themselves
and I scream, so the cry
would awaken me

I want to, I try to, I hope to
awake
but the dream does not disappear
all the more it intertwines
with the cry and the pain
and the more inexplicable the pain
the deeper seems the dream
and it is clear
this is not at all a dream
and there is no escape from it…

Listen to the Woodpecker at Your Temple

It is good always to be young
Like a woman
And not divide one's life
With childhood, maturity and old age
But divide it
With childhood maturity and old age.

Do not shoot at the falcon in the sky
It carries your thoughts
Do not frighten the nightingale
In your heart

Play with children
Speak seriously
With the elderly

Do not chase the firebird
Off your shoulders

Release the butterfly
From your hand—
It has its own truth

Listen to the woodpecker
At your temple

Rabbits

If rabbits were armed
to kill wolves
would the rabbits
having killed the wolves
kill one another?
Would the rabbits
kill those
who armed them?
Would there be
rabbits?

Sea of Life

In a sea of life
Time throws us
A reflecting net:

Our souls swim
Toward their reflection
The closer you see yourself
The further away you want
To swim

But you are already caught
And you wriggle
Not to escape
But to remain

The Sky

The sky will never
reflect itself
in a bowl of soup

The Bird Still Sings

The bird still sings
Beautifully and undisturbed
And girls already began to sing
Their song
Not one of which
They know to the end
And the sun cooled down
It cannot come
Listening it cannot depart

A Break

Distance between us
an expanse
an eternally
open wound

It heals gradually
in time
of our only
life

Diogenes

With a lantern
I am going
through
the forest:

oak tree
where is your
brother
deer

through
the village:

puppy
where is your
friend

through
the city:

people
where is
a human being

Invisible Brush Strokes

one hundred thirteen billion
three hundred ninety-four
million
seven thousand eight hundred
twenty-six
invisible brush strokes
nature needed
to sketch this landscape

the artist managed
only thirty-three
thousand
one hundred twelve strokes

and of the two hundred
fifty-five
visitors to the exhibit
only two
did not pass by the painting

and one of them
was amazed at the price
three thousand five hundred rubles
seemed to him
too much

Your Song

Your song
has been sung
my nightingale

Now begins the time
of wolf's howling
snake's hissing
hyena's laughter
crocodile's tears

And the lion's
share

from **TELESCOPE OF TIME** (2003)

And Finally We Have Freedom

and
finally we have
freedom
to think freely
but
there is no time
time is money

I Multiply

I multiply
in the viruses
of multiple
computers
in the darkness of various departments
under the oppression of personal
acts
in the offices of
secret consultations
directives by the committees
for special services

For all this general personnel
I hold no
responsibility

The Latest News

Europe is completely destroyed
Asia is ruined
Africa ravaged
Australia is trying to survive
America
according to the word from Asia
doesn't give any signs of life
the rest of America
refutes the report
whether such information
reached the remaining Europe
remains unconfirmed
and now about the weather
above the remaining earth
fog and fumes
but according to estimates
of extinct astrologers
the stars will continue
to forecast
a bright future

An Urgent Report

On the 17th of February
an old woman
boarded a bus
and said:
—Hello!

Mass Media

Global
Guff
Traverses
The great ocean

Intercontinental
Nonsense
Runs between
The east and the west

Super highways
Misunderstandings
Cross
All borders

The world's sense
Of moderation
Is in transatlantic
Trance

Request of the Witty

It is not necessary
to understand me
halfway

let me
finish

My Foreign Friends

my armenian friends
told me about the insidious atatürk
how he deceived russian lenin
and all of armenia

my azerbaijani friends
told me about the genial atatürk
how he brought new life
to his turkey

my georgian friends
did not speak about atatürk
only about the genial stalin
how he on time replaced
russian lenin

my russian friends
told me that lenin
is not altogether russian
and stalin not at all georgian

my azerbaijani friends
read to me in turkish
poems of the genial nâzim hikmet
about stone bronze plaster
paper stalin
who with his boots
trampled upon us all

my german friends
with knowledge of the affair
told me that my russian friends
all their life trampled upon my friends
georgians armenians azerbaijanis chechens
jews lithuanians latvians estonians
and a multitude of other nations
with their historical boots

lately it's not going
well in russia with boots
especially in demand
are german boots

Widening of the Universe

The earth flowers
like a violet
one from the other further apart
its petals
europe
asia
africa
america
australia

then they fly around

the people will be sad
about the beautiful departing spring
when they were separated
only by the seas
and borders

Strivings

A snowflake in the sky
seeks
on which land to fall

A girl seeks
in childhood
whom to love

Children seek
in all the eyes
to whom should they
be born

Gothic Churches

gothic churches
soar upward
toward the sky

they fly up
and return
with something

russian churches
under golden
parachute domes

already
landed

A Moment of Summer

A bird is not large
and grasses
for her are magic heaven
and through them
emerges descending sun
like
twinkling bonfire
in the outskirts of each blade
and the bird
gazing
cannot fly off

A Moment of Autumn

The forest burns
the leaves on trees
blaze
and through the trees one sees
how in the field
stands all autumn long
Mikhail Prishvin
and tries to persuade a titmouse
not to fire up
the sea

Disappearance

Disappearance. In time you
even miss a disappearing cloud. Disappearance
Of flowers disturbs a sensitive soul, though
The garden itself doesn't stir. Disappearance of
Snow on Bruegel the Elder's canvas
Would disturb more than disappearance of
Bruegel himself. Disappearance of leaves
With the coming of the wind. Disappearance of bread
From the table. Sudden disappearance
Of the table from the room, the room from its space.
Disappearance of a person, unnoticed by
The garden, table, space, time,
A human. Disappearance of humanity in
Human beings. Disappearance of love
In the beloved. Disappearance of it in the lover.
Disappearance of humans on earth, earth in the sky,
Sky in the disappearing soul, disappearance
Of lightning without the thunder.
Disappearance of a smile, not finding
A face. Happiness of disappearance,
Before everything disappears.

A Mistake

A poet all-seeing
discusses with the blind
visions for the future

all-knowing
questions the unknowing
about the unknown

and talks about everything
to the all-hearing

to hide it forever
from the deaf

Singing Lesson

Man
Invented a cage
Before
Wings

In cages
The winged sing
About the freedom
Of flight

In front of the cages
Sing those without wings
About the justice
Of cages

Poetry

Poetry
is natural
like a window in a house

artificial
like the glass in a window

unexpected
like the world beyond the window

regular
like science

appearing at the juncture
of dawnology
and
sunsetology

Freedom Epidemic

Freedom
epidemic:

The most dangerous
bacteria carriers
are people
who have recovered
from love

History of Mail

For 300 years
Russians claimed
oppression by the Mongols
who it turns out
were just delivering the mail
for 300 years
Russia received letters
it couldn't read
that's why Moscow
had to be burned intermittently
in order to free itself from the darkness
of unread letters

finally Ivan the Terrible
went East
took Kazan and began
to send letters West
to the runaway Prince Kurbskoy
these terrible letters
were answered by Peter the Great
from Holland overseas

then Catherine also the Great
arranged a connection with the better world
of Mr. Voltaire and Napoleon
the very Bonaparte in continuous burning
of Moscow helped introduce
the elegant French epistolary style
for nobility so as not to confuse
the common folk
too early with
freedom equality and fraternity

with better delivery of mail
Decembrists sent their letters
about reforming Russia
from Siberia to awaken
Herzen in London
they were answered by
Vladimir Ilych squinting
his far-sighted Mongolian gaze
from Geneva from Zurich

and the October Revolution
came to pass
as an inevitable consequence
of Mongolian mail
as an Eastern
reply and a challenge to the West

in the next 300 years
something will come to us as a response
from the West
by electronic mail

Drawing Lession – 1

Pushkin before death
longed for cloudberries
draw
a cloudberry

draw
the forbidden fruit
before which there was
immortality

draw
the apple of discord
before which there were
no wars

draw
the essential
fruits of enlightenment
which are always in need

but when we have them
we will
live
our genuine life

and die
only our own
death

Geography Lesson

Give a clue to the silent one
where the borders of earth and mind are:
a limited student
cannot live without a clue

give a clue for the way of connecting
a God-forsaken place and
the Promised Land

about Wonderland:
how many rivers of sweat and blood
fall into the sea of Bliss
what's the quantity of armed forces
in the other world

whisper a clue: we
are ready to leave behind us
only blank space

give a clue out loud: we must
find within ourselves
the poles of good and hope

give a clue in chorus: the earth
has the form of an air balloon
and is held
by our word of honor

Anatomy Lesson

Forgive me
students
but my skeleton
will not be
a good visual aid

while still alive
I so loved life and freedom
that I opened up my chest
to free my heart
and from each rib
tried
to create a woman

while alive I used to
tear my brain apart
with questions about life

not to mention
my skull

Pity

I pity the Russians. Their tears
Drain into the Caspian Sea.
I pity the Jews. The smoke of their fatherland
Burns the eyes. I pity the Germans, because
No one pities them. I pity
The Neanderthals. Dying they
Believed in man. I pity
The Americans. They, it seems,
Pity no one. I pity
The Aborigines. They are concealed in modern
Dress. Navigators I pity for
Invariably they'll stumble on land.
I pity the geographers. They
Don't see the earth behind the globe.
I pity the astronomers. All their hope
Lies in the night.
I pity the historians, for they
Cannot invent
A better history...

Russia's Dream

Russia sleeps in a cold dew
and dreams
that she is America:
her chatterers are congressmen
her loafers are the unemployed
her hooligans are gangsters
her drunkards are drug addicts
her profiteers are businessmen
her Russians are Blacks
and she must fly to the Moon

Russia awakens in a cold sweat
everything appears to be in its place
chatterers are chatterers
loafers are loafers
hooligans are hooligans
Russians are Russians
only she must land
in the right place

and Russia again falls asleep
and within her awakens the Russian idea—
that America sleeps and dreams
that it is Russia

Face

into my face
I have absorbed
the faces of
all those I love

who will tell me
I am not handsome

Laughter 1971

I laugh
to myself
because I hear
them laughing
at us

they are laughing at us
because they see
what we are
laughing at

saddest of all
is the one who wants
to laugh
last

it is funny
to wait
that long

A Terrible Tale

Terrible times
Recede further and further
And stumble
Upon the time of first love
From which we were born

They receded into the past
In fear
Swapping their fears
With other terrible times
They became even more terrible

One looks at the other
Wide-eyed
Inciting one another
Whether to wait for the confusion
Or turn
Into the present

Let the time
Of first love
Protect us forever

Points of View

Man doesn't spin a web
because he's afraid of
flies
posed a spider

Man doesn't spin a web
because he's afraid of
spiders
thought a fly

Man doesn't spin a web
thought a web
because he has already spun
so much
he fears himself

What did I get myself into
thinks
man

It seems quite odd
To be with some people

With some
I feel
Like a diamond
Swallowed
By a hen

Another looks at me
And I feel
Like a hen
Which swallowed
A diamond

Of course
Best of all is to be
With those with whom
I can relate as a diamond
To a diamond

But in time
There are fewer and fewer
Of those with whom
I can simply
Speak as a hen
To a hen

Ode to Time

Oh!
Oh, half past six!
Oh, quarter to seven! Oh, five to!
Oh, seven in the morning!
Oh, eight! Oh, nine! Oh, ten!
Oh, eleven, twelve, one!
Oh, lunch break! Oh, after-
Lunch break! Oh,
After the afternoon
Nap of a faun! Oh, the latest news hour!
Oh, horror! Oh, supper hour! Oh, already
The last straw! Oh, the last cloud
Of the dispersing storm! Oh, the last
Leaf! Oh, the last day
Of Pompeii! Oh, never!
Oh, after the flood! Oh, half
Past eleven! Oh, five to!
Oh, midnight!
Oh, midday!
Oh, midnight!
Oh, hit! Oh, miss!
Oh, Moscow time!
Oh, Greenwich time!
Oh, for whom the bell tolls!
Oh, the hours strike! Oh, the happy ones!
Oh, half past six!
Oh, midday!
Oh, midnight!
Oh, five to!

Oasis of Time

In the desert of space
an oasis of time is
a clear source
of inspiration

we look at it
as into a mirror

we take in
what we
see

to have the strength
to go
where there is nothing to see

Globe – 1961

Ah, that globe,
My little one!
Ah, how it behaved,
When they led it
To the execution:
It was singing!
At the same time
It scratched its
Bald
Northern spot!
And at once
Pieces of icicles
flew in all directions…
And at once all shouted:
Aha, we told you that
it would create
the next
ice age!

Creation

Creating lyrics
in the epoch of epic literature

creating tragedy
in the epoch of ode

creating man
in the epoch of humanism

creating good
in the epoch of goodness

creating one's own
in the epoch of mastery

creating strangeness
in the epoch of computation

creating
in the epoch of creation

amidst permissible miracles
forever create

impermissible
miracle

Contemporary Man – 2

Contemporary man
extends himself through the wire
together with the murmur of the sea
jams himself into the shell of the telephone
compresses himself
seeks immortality
on a compact disc
becomes a sea monster
a prisoner of the television aquarium
he becomes more portable
more compact
more contemporary
already he can be switched on
switched off
made louder softer
he doesn't see you
doesn't hear you
he doesn't know you

Word's Torture

From the silence of feeling
and the mind's will
is born silver—
a word.
It learns to walk
in time.
It learns to stand on its own
in space.
It learns to fly
in the mind.

Silver, from which life is coined
lines of eternity,
silver,
in response to its call
one may hear
the same good word,
at the sound of which
important people and tamed beasts
turn around,
elephants and whales
bow before it—
because for ages
the purpose of words
has been to hold the Earth,
and the purpose of man
to keep
the Word.

To the Statisticians

Be more interested
in the quantity
of souls
per head
of population

the quantity of brains
per head

the quantity of ideas
per brain

the quantity of opinions
per idea

the quantity of rumors
per opinion

the quantity
of lies
per quantity
of truth

be more interested
in conversion of quantity
into quality

Sensations of the Century

romantic minds of calculators
confirm
that the earth was visited by aliens
from outer space
otherwise
who would have evolved
ape
into man

sensible high officials
little by little.
regulate information
about the flying saucers
which appear above the earth
to the hungry children of a glutted planet

flighty people
in california and the pamirs
seek
the abominable snowman

a human
unquestionably
unavoidably
must be found

Landscape with Polyphemus

All this is reflected:

Sisyphus is pushing his rock
Icarus is falling into the sea
Prometheus is chained to a cliff

while indifferent nymphs
apolitical fauns
rollick carelessly
in ecstasy
of a fleeting life

all this is reflected
in the bloodshot
single eye of Polyphemus

that is just about to be gouged
by a wanderer
seeking his homeland
Odysseus

World Market

the past
is more expensive

they don't display it in the window
they lock it up in the drawer
for connoisseurs

in exchange for an armful of the present
they give a pinch
of the dubious past

to the inexperienced they whisper:
now there is a good past
enough
for a lifetime

who
has
the future

Small Homeland

When the homeland is near—
one isn't anxious – one
doesn't fly like a leaf
that carries
its own roots

If the homeland is distant
in recollection
it becomes all the more puzzling:
if before
one dreamed about faraway places
now
one imagines one's own country

After
decades one stands
on the ground of childhood steps
under the shade of childhood palms—
there is your home

Your home
is strong
in it lived your silence
and it endured
your first
word

With an Unarmed Eye

Looking at the stars
from the earth
I don't believe a star
is an eternal flame—
a memorial
of an unknown planet

I hope
that no one's life has faded
for the sake of their distant luster
that no one has burned in darkness
for the sake of their majestic light

That no one
seized land
from anyone
for the sake of their
airless
expanse

Temporary Pleasures

the spring of humanity
is arriving
all want
to play in green grass
no one wants
to plow and sow

the morning of humanity
is arriving
all want
to receive love letters
no one wants
to deliver the mail

eternity is arriving
all shout
freeze
this moment

no one
wants
to waste
their time

People's Hearts

people's hearts
yearn for each other
but their path is blocked
by passports
wallets
tickets

people's hands
reach out to each other
but they are pulled away
by shopping bags
briefcases
with business papers
watches
that are always fast

people want
to go to each other
but they are carried away
by trains airplanes
hemispheres on the globe
falling away from each other

the border between which
is in the heart
of every one
of us

With a Wave of My Hand

With a wave of my hand
I draw
you
standing against the dark horizon
in full height

airless expanse
between us
is carved out
by the gravitation of our lips:

here forms
a single inevitable
word
which may be uttered

only
in unison

A Sentence

This sentence
is a good preposition
to offer you a proposition

I – the subject
love – the predicate
you – the object
most direct

You the pronoun
a place for my love
you are a part of my anxious utterance
a singular number
upon which the world descended

You are
my second face
look at me with love
without you
I simply don't have a face

Poetic Videoclip – 1

wind wind white snow
Blok listens to the music of revolution
in a yellow jacket red like the Marseillaise
out of the snowdrift appears the beautiful
one hundred twenty-two-year-old Mayakovsky
upon meeting him
the sky takes off its hat
from ancient times
Barkov appears drunk
he takes off his antique trousers
relieves himself into the hat
Barkov and Mayakovsky
stand almost next to each other
Blok sings in a voice
made of velvet from Mayakovsky's trousers
we will fan the world's flames
Mayakovsky and Barkov without trousers
burn Blok's library
Blok sings
man doesn't stand on legs
Barkov sings
the affair is done

Poetic Videoclip – 2

marx dressed as beethoven
plays the appassionata
lenin with a tied up cheek
enchantingly listens exclaims
what experienced human being appears
out of the snowdrift in a yellow jacket
red as the *marseillaise*
122-year-old mayakovsky
he shouts in terror
lenin!!! is alive!!!
after death we stand
almost next to each other
he at "l" and i at "m"
from under the piano appears esenin
he sings in kid gloves
for me lenin is not an icon either
out of the snowdrift from under the piano
appears a predatory beast
with red flags
it throws flags and banners
it throws itself on esenin
esenin tries to sing
i never hit our smaller
brothers on the head
the beast hits esenin on the head
out of the beautiful mayakovsky appears
wrinkled pasternak
pasternak sings not in his own voice
i am alone everything is sinking

out of lenin's mummy appears
like an insect from a larva
a mummy of comrade stalin
it sings with a voice of marx and beethoven
there ain't no other writers

Poetic Videoclip – 3

Hava Nagila plays
the music of perestroika
Gorbachov and Thatcher listen
Evtushenko sings in a yellow American jacket
having appeared out of the snowdrift
a poet in a den is larger than a bear
a choir of Chechens under the direction of Kobzon
sings let a great country rise
out of the snowdrift appears
a man who looks like False Dmitri
Aleksandrovich Prigov in a police uniform
Evtushenko in fear disappears
Chechens run for the hills
Kobzon convincingly sings
in this is our strength
Prigov calls the spirit
of capricious Goya
where are Goi?
after death we stand
almost next to each other
he on "G" and I on "G"
out of the den appears the poet Goya
I am Goya
all in fear disperse
Goya sings
a bear in Russia is more than a bear

Clip – 4

after death
all lie
almost
next to each other

Non-Contemporary Person

we live – we breathe
a day passes
thanks be to God

outside an old woman
tells another

I am
holding
my breath

Economized Man

Unexpectedly I dreamt
I was
an economized
man

take me people
I am yet another
economized man!

if the people answer
all the same
we are not enough for you
many of us have been wasted
on you already

I extend my economized arms
I lower my economized head

don't be discouraged! – other
economized people shout to me—
we'll find a use for you!

they pat me
on my economized back
and I awaken

it's time
to waste myself
further

The Toothless

the toothless
hurry to lisp the truth
that's stuck in their throat

lies
fastened to their teeth
fall out together with the teeth

listen
to the speech of the toothless

and translate it
into the language
of the sharp-tongued

Snow

snow was sent to earth so no one would think the air is
immaterial
so no one would think the wind is futile
snow assures us
that the earth is dazzling like the sky
even more dazzling
especially in the moonlight
when it is evident that our earth is a precious jewel
that can shine on everyone's eyelashes
snow covers the roads so that we remain
with those around us
snow melts on our eyes
so we do not forget
that everything fascinating is transient
snow lies over fields of unread books
snow squeaks beneath the footsteps of the universe

Report on the Senses

Sense of moderation
hindered sense of humor
in manifesting its senses

Sense of humor
challenged sense of moderation
to a duel

Sense of moderation
assessed humor
and expressed sympathy
at which sense of humor
lost its senses

Sense of moderation
from sense of duty
brought it to its senses

From accepted measures
sense of humor
became moderate

Sense of moderation
expressed sincerely:
we are happy
we haven't lost
sense of humor!

Sense of Humor

Praise
the head of family
who declares from now on
there's nothing to eat at home
with such a sense of humor
the children burst out
in laughter

Praise
the head of state
who declares to the people
war has begun
with such a sense of humor
that armed to their teeth
people's teeth begin to fall out from laughter

Praise
the head of judiciary
who declares a sense of humor
to be the holy duty of each
proper
citizen

The Art of Firing

perfect the art of firing
try more precisely
not to hit a human being
neither a man because he is going toward a woman
nor a woman because she is going toward a child
nor a child because it doesn't know yet where to go
nor an elder because he wants
to meet only his own death

carefully perfect
the art of bombing
it is so difficult
not to hit a city or touch a village
not to erase from the face of the earth
one more uncommon expression
perfect this art
for the sake of someone's or your own life

for bullets and bombs may miss you
but you will still have to escape the mines
only because
your perfect enemy
doesn't want to cede to you
in this striking art

Silence – 1

silence
approaches
the heart
even deeper

already
are heard
the beats
of unstressed
vowels
of the unutterable
d

Chinese Motif

I do not ascribe
to the limits
of serene
landscapes

the wind
is blowing from the hills

I am sinking
into the seas and rivers

I take hold of the brush
and fade
into the sky

Fear

I am afraid
that the terror
from the past
will return

I am afraid
that the terror
will suddenly appear
in the future

I am afraid
of the present
fear

afraid
that fear
will not help

Dark People

darkness
gives rise to
rumors

rumors
influence
tastes

tastes
influence
attitudes

in the world are such attitudes
as is
the world

Moon

moon
turned over
is moon

medal
turned over
is heart

heart
turned over
is blood

blood
turned over
is water

water
turned over
is tears

tears
are laughter
turned over

life is death
turned over
life

don't turn over
look at everything
from the beginning

Flight of the Russian Soul

Is it easy for you to be free,
O Russian soul?
Or do those lingering Russian songs
which lure one so far without letting go,
refuse to release you?
Did the air in the womb
of world spirit seem
of non-Russian fragrance?
Among heavenly birds,
ground beetles, moths
appear fleeting
German, Japanese,
naive souls,
implicated, strange,
and do you, incomprehensible to them,
frightfully fly by
like a nightingale whistle?
If the souls cry in unison,
how deep you are and transparent!
If the souls laugh in unison,
you are the most breathless of them all,
O flying Russian soul!
And so, finally, free,
in longed-for freedom,
in space, wider than a field,
without body chains, in the clouds, scaling
all the news, except
the good ones, exfoliating everything
earthly, everything past, or everything
future, or are you

simply litotes of the Russian soil,
and where is it—
the Russian sky?

Golden Autumn

It seems too many words
were thrown to the wind
so the wind is piercing

it seems too often
they were off the mark
so the sky is cloudy

it seems for too many
it's burning under their feet
so the leaves are glowing

it seems a lot of water has flowed
since we failed to find common ground
so the water freezes

how many more talents
must be buried in the cold earth
so spring
will appear again?

Weeping

I weep
because no one
sees

I weep
because no one
hears

I weep
because no one believes
in tears

I weep
because everything
passes

even
weeping

Twilight of Vanity

every night
the corpse
lifts up
the gravestone
and checks by feeling

whether the name
on the stone
has rubbed off

Wanted Time

wanted a face
for the removal
of a golden mask

wanted a man
for making a creator
in his own image

wanted hunters
for capturing
such a man

the price per head
will be announced
separately

Ecology

from the experience of transformation
of nature
I realize that it's harmful
to dry up the marshes
of unpleasant thoughts

for nature's balance
may be destroyed
with the extinction of nonsense
which hovers over mental
quagmire

what may evaporate
are the running waters of clear thinking
from where rare and clear thoughts
are derived

by computers
of a generation wishing to survive

Golden Man

acquaintances
befriend him
non-acquaintances
want to be acquainted

day and night
they hang around him
business-like people with shovels
look at him
with reproach

business-like people with shovels
have a
dual mission:
bury him publicly
and secretly
dig him up
again

they noticed
in his heart
deposits of gold

Telescope of Time

from deep
grasses infused by the sun
from the earth
alone already almost earth
you look at the clear sky
in daylight you try to foresee the stars

as if from an old age
childhood
is so high up!

Siberian Sun

life goes from east to west
I awaken
it is still so quiet
one can hear
how at the shore of the Okhotsk sea
children play
at recess

it is still so dark
one can see
from the heights of Moscow University
how from the depths appears
the Siberian sun

Silence – 2

unheard silence
reaches
even
to the stars
like old trees
fall into childhood
clinging
while playing with their
annual rings

Fairy Birds

fairy birds
play with rain

they are like princesses on a pea
spinning on the flying drops

others as if on wire
try to sit
on the slant line of rain

some
at breakneck speed
leap into the apertures of lightning
and appear
beyond the heaven

these are the most educated
the rain reminds them
of a cage

Hypothesis About Man

No matter how much they stress
that man is a natural being
experience shows that man
from the primitive to the man of the future
is an invented being
designed for further inventions
in no case premeditated
so well designed
that he doesn't have to think
think up and think through
sometimes even over generations
after all the natural art of thinking
is an eternal blessing and a burden
to each man in a generation
to each generation in history
to all together and to each separately
(whoever thinks otherwise
thank you also
for thinking)

Zoshchenko's Dream

before sunrise
the sea waves
come to the shore
as huge fiery tigers

tigers enter my home
they bring into it
the smell of the sun and the sea

they save me
from a crowd of melancholy beggars
at my doors

the beggars at my doors
don't allow me
to go out
to the sea

In Memory of Sea Waves

in memory of sea waves
the middle ages under sails
passed without a trace
(not considering sunken treasures)
ancient worlds on oars
pre-history passed without a trace
(not considering sunken continents)
waves of geographic discoveries
made noise only on land
the sea does not change
no matter how many lashes
or showers with bombs
(including the deep ones)
the sea doesn't remember anything
and we
some a little deeper some less so
go through life carefree
into the shaken undisturbed waters

Desert

desert
is a disgraced embassy of the sun
a depository of mirages
an embodiment of an ancient dream of hills
rocking like the sea

at night each of the visible stars
chooses for itself a grain of sand
and throws it from sunray to sunray saying
this one is mine

invisible stars stir in invisible height
pleading to the visible stars—
go away
we can't see a thing
we want to throw our own grain of sand

during the day all the grains are in the embrace of the sun
which feels equal only to the desert

not to the sea
which is too absorbed with itself

for the wise the desert
is not only a place
where there's something to think about

it's a space for thoughts about that
which is worth
imagining

Shark – 1

one night it swims up
to your headboard
and opens wide its jaws:

the iron frame
of the soldier's bed
saves you

at dawn you dream
how good it is that you
are a soldier
sleeping on a reliable
iron bed

in the morning a different iron
lies in wait for you

Shark – 2

night is the sea
at night you cannot hide from it
it swims up without a sound
and opens wide its jaws

not to devour you
but to expel from its belly
what it devoured earlier

feeling yourself still alive
in terror and hope
you extricate yourself from the tangle
of dead octopuses
you shake off the fish scales
from the remains
of an unhappy diver

God forbid
another night
like this one

Russian Question

Kalashnikov?
Baryshnikov?
Baryshnikov?
Kalashnikov?

Baryshnikov?
Kalashnikov?
Kalashnikov?
Baryshnikov?

Kalashnikov?
Baryshnikov?
Kalashnikov?

Baryshnikov?
Kalashnikov?
Baryshnikov?

A Gathering of Watches

Here is a watch that forever points to midnight
Here is a watch that fell into the sea and dissolved
Here is a watch that wakes you up as soon as you fall asleep
Here is a watch, more like the moon, but small, because it's at the end
of the world
A watch like a watermelon, from which they swallowed time
A watch which bursts as soon as you wind it up
A watch which ticked for so long, it turned into a woodpecker and sat
upon a tree
A watch threateningly repetitive: your hour has struck!
A watch in the shape of a cat in a bag for those who love freedom:
you can select from it any hour at random
But the watch which is dearest to me: the one by which I waited for
you, and you still
haven't come, I shake it from time to time and wear it

Wild West

Over there far away
that is all europe
that is where the serbs sing
where the english from all of england swim to america
where the french in chorus daily take on the bastille
where the spanish dance and avenge the hijacking of europe
where the germans shuffle papers and run for health
where the swiss have a hole in their cheese
where the dutch with hope await invasions by don quixotes
where the swedes visit the danes
where the italians jump on their one leg
where the poles still haven't disappeared
where the turks quietly reconstruct their byzantium
where the russians cannot decide
where they are and want to be europe

Beloved

beloved
do not fear
I did not hang myself
it is my topcoat
that got caught on a bough
where we were sitting

beloved
do not worry
I was not beheaded
it is just my hat
the cold wind
chases behind you

beloved
do not stop
I will not drown
what was I to do
without a hat and a topcoat
but jump off the bridge
into the water

A Lesson in Math

From a desert
we subtract a desert—
and get
a field

A steppe
we raise a step—
and get
a yard

We put together
yards and fields—
and get
fruits and bread

We divide—
and get
friends

We multiply—
and get
life.

Poems Fly Up Into the Sky like Airplanes

Poems fly up into the sky like airplanes
They easily go up into the clouds
They are not touched by lightning
They are not frightened by thunder
They are not afraid of the night
Birds and stars have something in common with them
They smash to smithereens
Descending onto a white sheet of paper

Translation of Poetry

The flash of birds' flight
Translates to the somnolent scurrying of the fish

And back

From the ancient language of fish
To the contemporary syntax of the birds' flight

And so on

From the dark language of the ocean
To the clear language of the sky

And back

Song of Odysseus

When my ship comes in,
A song will come ashore with me,
To which until then only the sea was listening,
For the song was competing with the call of the sirens.
It will have only soft vowel sounds,
That sound that way in the pale translation
From the language of roaming to the language of mooring:

I love you with the hoarse cry of the seagulls,
With the scream of the eagles, flying toward the scent of Prometheus'
liver,
With the thousand-faced silence of the sea turtle,
With the click of the sperm whale that wants to be a roar,
With the pantomime, executed by the tentacles of the octopus,
Before which all seaweeds stand on end.

I love you with all my body coming from the sea,
With all its rivers, tributaries of the Amazon and the Mississippi,
With all those deserts, which think themselves seas,
You can hear their sand sift through my desiccated throat.

I love you with all my heart, lungs and medulla,
I love you with the earth's crust and the star-studded sky,
With the fall of waterfalls and the conjugation of verbs,
I love you with the invasion of Europe by the Huns,
With the Hundred Years' War and the Mongolian Horde,
With the uprising of Spartacus and the Great Migration,
With Alexander's column and the Tower of Pisa,
With the speed of the Gulf Stream warming the North Pole.

I love you with the letter of the law of gravity
And the verdict of the death penalty,
Unto-the-death penalty through the eternal fall
Into your bottomless Bermuda triangle.

From the Seventh Heaven

From the seventh heaven
the last verities
fly to us with hope

but they always burn out
in the dense layers
of our intractable atmosphere
their extinguished brilliance awakening in us
inspiration

for our new illusions

from **CONTRADICTIONS** (2019)

A Lake in the Mountains

A tectonic break
suddenly an abyss unfolds
and everything fills with clear water
(water in the depth, depth in the water)
in it the sky reflects incessantly
perhaps in hope to wash off the stars
perhaps it is here it catches the stars
all that is missing is a woman bathing
though it would be quite cold for her
perhaps she would cry out from the cold
perhaps she would be terrified by the depth
terrified as it seems
in the bottomless funnel of my memory
where so much water has flowed
and she is there alone
hopelessly forgotten by me
though it is mainly because of her
that there still reflects the sky

Experience

During my whole
long life
night darkness
has not altered

but it appears
to me
that the stars
have become
more attentive
to each other

Moon's Steps

1.

Only those in love, dear moon,
may step over you—
they know
the value of your light
and will not frighten
your fireflies

2.

This night
when all the flowers are white
when all the windows are open
I am going toward your window
over the earth
quietly
at the speed of the moon's light

Illumination

all the time you wait for an exceptional idea
which will change the whole world
to yourself you go intensely over
all common ideas
that are not changing the world

look how they run away from you:
you already emit smoke
you have overheated yourself

you are probably on the right path:
soon you will be on fire
if you can withstand the heat
of an uncommon idea

you still don't know what kind of an idea it is
but you imagine its appearance
illumination:

the head shines like the sun
you are blinded
others have seen the light
you have burned to the ground
with confidence
in the transformation of the world

Average Life

An amazing sensation
of average life

someone walks
above your head
you walk
above heads of others
looking at the ceiling
you sigh – the sky
looking at the floor
you repeat – the earth
you grieve
for not having seen a soul
on your own horizon

My Tongue

My tongue—
having survived
the tower of Babel
and all
ivory towers
now lies dumb
under the yoke
of the television
tower

Re-evaluation of Value

They say
that in time
everything will be simpler

Heads torn off
will be sorted out—
these here were torn off
according to the law, this one
was without a tsar in the head,
and this one
simply turned up under
arm,
while this one
was real brains—
and this one too!

Onto headless models
they will manufacture visual
aids
for high schools
in which the teachers
in order to save their
heads
will teach future
heads of children:
in time
everything will be simpler.

Heads also.

The Last Day

On the third
day
the dove
returned
to Noah's
ark
with a bomb
in its beak

There is no land yet
but already there is
air

Alternative History

Here is what it could have been:
Genghis Khan defeated Alexander
Or Tamerlane defeated Napoleon
Or Napoleon defeated Tamerlane
Or Attila defeated Caesar
Or still more than this
Forty thousand Genghis Khans
Against forty thousand Napoleons
Or one hundred thousand Alexanders
Against one hundred thousand Tamerlanes
Or a million of Peters
Against millions of Alexanders
And in that all are equally armed
Or in general equally unarmed
And then in general some six billion
Let it be seven billion participants
Against eight or ten billion observers

Western Landscape

Windmills
windmills
windmills

confident
rotation
of contemporary
sails

ecologically friendly energy
in homes of good-hearted
citizens

nostalgia
for Don Quixote

Optimistic Geography

North America
still hasn't slipped
into South America

Asia Major
still hasn't crushed
Central and Asia Minor

Europe still hasn't fallen
through the Mediterranean
onto free Africa

Africa still
hasn't been swallowed
by the Sahara

Icebergs of Antarctica
still haven't merged
with the ice
of Greenland

Forces of gravity
still surpass
any
armed forces

The physical map
still hasn't destroyed
the political map of the world

Mediocrity

Mediocrity
of state importance
Stupidity
of historical world significance
Deception
of the first degree

there are interesting facts
that should be silenced
or put to careful scrutiny
by means of free
mass information

in narrow circles
of minds endlessly appearing
under the threat of loss
it is acceptable to suppose

that incompetence of state importance
is stupidity
of historical world significance
which if silenced
is deception
of the first degree

Do Not Frighten the Moon

Do not frighten the moon
when at the end of the night
a sleepwalker appears in the light

Do not ask him
where he is from or where he is going
what he needs
at the end of the night
what he dreams
at the end of his life

O how dangerous
are the moments
when in light
we are visible
to everyone

Song of the Wolf

I am the wolf wolf
I am the winter night wolf wolf
My footsteps serve the spirit of snow
I am the master of crackling someone's bones
It was I who blew freezing stars
Upon your window pane
While you slept in a dream
I howled the full moon into the sky
When you still couldn't look up at the sky
It was I who taught you to fear evening trees
It was I who charmed you from dangerous games with one's shadow
It was I who prompted you to be in the pack

I am the wolf wolf
I am the winter night wolf
I am going from you into your winter tale

Song of the Tiger

I am the tiger
I am the thunder of taiga and the lightning of the jungle
Once when there still was a lot of fire
And still very little water
I came out of the fire alive
And began to grow plants around me
So they would reflect in my green eyes
But you should not meet my gaze
For my gaze is set at the edge of my teeth
And do not follow my tracks
For I am always behind you
And I despise man
For he is only the master of domestic cats

The Dancing Bear

I put my left foot forward
I put my right foot forward
I put my left foot backward
I put my right foot backward
I pretend I am going forward
I pretend I am going backward
You would say these were paws
I would say they are hands
I spread my hands
I put my hands together
I raise the wind
I lower the wind
Under my feet the damp earth rotates
But it doesn't disappear
The sky spins above my head
But it doesn't disappear
The trees go around me
But they cannot entwine me
The birds are silent while I dance
Afraid that I might take flight
The grass grows while I dance
Afraid that I might fall
The birds are silent but not without reason
After all I might start to sing
And the grass grows without reason
After all I won't fall I am not a man

Risk of Peace

Autumn trees risk blossoming every spring
risk of blossoming
mortals risk giving birth to mortals
in pursuit of fantastic immortality
risk of birth
this risk is justified by the unity of life
its incredible mastery of the times
spaces
risk of life
which is justified by life itself
and that is why on every living planet
against the risk of war and enmity
accumulates the risk of peace
the risk of peace and trust
which in counterbalance to the risk of war and death
is justified by life
not only by life which began history
but also
by life which only will come
which only will come then
when we all collect our senses to allow ourselves
not the endless yoke of defense
but the risk of trusting peace
the mortal risk
of peace

Enemy Image

Who knows what kind of bloody battles
lead bloodless microbes with viruses,
how one featureless form
swallows up another
without losing its form or finding one,
but how do they without eyes and ears
determine without error
the enemy's image,
that has neither eyes, nor ears,
how do they win,
not having a mouth, to shout hurrah,
they don't die
but only pass from one gut to another,
digging up horror for victory
already over us
carelessly
having set up our mind's eyes and ears
in search of a keen and sighted
awful and essential
enemy image,
according to our own
frightful image and likeness.

Sunset at Sea

The sun sets into the sea
brighter than on the horizon
it begins to expand in size
absorbing its own reflection

It doesn't want to leave
and it's embarrassed
it cannot stay

The less time remains for it
to be between the sky and the sea
the more it expands

Finally the sea cuts
and shrinks it to a speck
now already together with the sky
the sea darkens not understanding
why it took part in this
so impetuously.

Despot's Clay Army

Chinese despot Qin Shi Huang
In the Second century Before the Common Era
Ordered all wise books burned
And all scholars and poets buried alive
And in his tomb
Hid in ambush
An army of terra cotta warriors
In case the people became wiser.
But with the passage of time
All the wisdom in books was restored
By those who memorized the books
And I had a terrible clay dream
That the despot's clay warriors
Came to our Twenty-first century
By the invisible silk, tea and clay road
Over the already discovered Pamirs and Urals
To our Russian land
To lock up our Russian books
And bury in our Russian soil
All who are still able to think
But they came, it seems, in vain
For all this was already done
By simple Russian
Contemporary wooden matryoshkas
And simple Russian
Children's clay whistles.
And no one is able to restore our wisdom
Since no one
Memorized anything.

Miluo, China – November 4, 2019

Miracle of Music

Astonishing miracle of music
Summoned only by ten fingers
Which must be able
In collision with white and black
To release colorful sounds
For all to hear
Without suspecting
In what outer darkness
They had been confined

2022

"Burich Unbound"
by
Vyacheslav Kupriyanov

On the 75th Anniversary of Vladimir Burich's Birth, The Founder of Contemporary Russian Free Verse (*Vers Libre*) —August 6, 2007

Twice I had to wait for the casket with the body of Burich arriving from Macedonia. The airplane landed at Sheremetevo airport on time; everyone alive had gone through customs already. "There was no casket from Skopje, but there is an unclaimed casket from Canada, if you would like," the airport crew kindly informed me. Perhaps Burich is alive after all.

Finally, the organizers of the Struga Poetry Evenings[1] called. It appears that the casket could not be loaded onto the Macedonian aircraft; it would arrive in three days by Aeroflot. Instead of bringing the casket directly to the car, the driver of the truck swung it in a circle, worrying about payment, which had already been given to his co-worker. It was the end of August 1994.

Then we recalled what Burich said to one of us on the street before departure: "I am going to Macedonia to die." But a day before departure he and I sat together with the Russian American from San Francisco, the Second Wave emigrant poet Ivan Burkin. We drank plenty of vodka and chased it down with cognac. After midnight, I escorted Burich on foot at a fast clip from Dinamo to the airport (as he feared going alone), because I still wanted to make it to the Metro.[2] He did not plan to die. But he often feared. In Dubrovnik[3] we were crossing a bridge over a precipice and he said to me, clutching my shoulder, "Hold me tighter!" He was afraid of heights. In the cozy German town of Bad Urach where, by the way, Slavic writing began, a local pastor and I floundered in warm baths in an open-air pool, while Burich, lifting his coat collar, strolled in the park nearby: he was afraid of water. He was afraid but not only for himself. Then on the way from Dubrovnik to Budva,[4] our bus suddenly hit a boy on a bike. Volodya,[5] sitting in front of me in terror, blocked my view and shouted, "Slava,[6] don't look!" In about an hour the whole bus (Croats and Serbs) gaily applauded the news that the boy was alive. And then came a poem published posthumously, "Highway Dubrovnik – Budva." Here are the last two lines:

In a puddle of the cyclist's spilled blood
reflects the setting sun

I cannot say that these lines were successful, not because the incident itself was unpleasant, but because free verse should not be inspired by an incident – its power is not in the observation of an event. Therefore, the best of Burich's poems are those in which there is a concrete expression of the abstract, or the ones that are a "condensation" of the understood subject. Since free verse must not describe a subject, but present in words some new subjectivity, revelations in free verse are rather difficult for the author. That is why I understood Burich's fear about his authorship – he feared to have his poems read before they were published. And that was so for all of his life. Wearily he went to public readings; it was always necessary to drag him there. He was leery of plagiarism as well as the illusion of plagiarism. Once he was enraged when he read a poem by Arvo Mets,[7] finding in it an elaboration of his own following poem:

A little girl's face is a meadow
A girl's face is a garden
A woman's is a home
A home full of worries

And here is a more "perceptive" Arvo Mets:

Young girls'
faces resemble
the sky,
the wind,
the clouds.
Then they become
devoted wives,
whose faces resemble
homes,
furniture,
shopping bags.
But their daughters'
faces again resemble
the sky, the wind
and streams of spring.

I want to believe there is confluence here of the principles of a semantic line. In Burich, everything is brought to an algebraic formula, in which all reductions and explanations are produced in parentheses. In Mets, rather than algebra, there is an aquarelle in which a whole catalogue of topics is written. Yet, while in Burich everything ends with a "home" (within one life), in Mets for this there is its own gentle "but" – an exit beyond the generational boundary. Once while reading my text, Burich, out of despair, ran barefoot out of the house into the snow. Here are the two texts in parallel for comparison:

Vladimir Burich	Vyacheslav Kupriyanov

BLACK AND WHITE

Black	*White*
seeks white	*fights with black*
to kill in it the light	*to death*
and turn it into grey	*to lie upon its bones*

I left out of my text the dedication to V.B. with whom it was published, to appease the addressee. If I may now reveal myself, I see here a difference in the view of the world in general. Burich, as I already mentioned, reduces, and I attempt to find an exit in the dead end, i.e., the light. I never, or almost never, quarreled with Burich, even though we held completely opposite views of the world. We had one and the same mission: to promote Russian free verse.

Together we went to discussion groups, though they did not invite us, as at the "Problems of Literature" in 1971, (but they did publish us together with our "opponents" Boris Slutsky[8] and David Samoylov[9]). Or they invited us, as at the "Foreign Literature" meeting in 1972, but did not publish us (since we did not register, as Pavel Toper[10] said). Andrei Sergeev[11] also did not register, having assigned free verse as an irregular unrhymed dol'nik.[12] In both publishing houses where he worked, Vladimir Burich experienced satisfaction by pinning up on official shelves his "Typological Table of Russian Poetic Speech." In it, like in Mendeleev's Table, free verse has its lawful place. At the "Foreign Literature" meeting David Samoylov, already at the beginning of our discussion, got up and called the forthcoming dispute incompetent, insignificant, and left, at what the discussion leader, experienced diplomat Nikolai Fedorenko,[13] expressed regret. When Vladimir Burich's turn came to take the podium with his "Table of Russian Poetic Speech," he passed by Slutsky's table who loudly whispered to his female colleague: "This poet is a Whitmanist!" It sounded evil enough, though Burich insisted that he himself came up with this word, as an admirer and follower of Whitman. Burich had his own expression: "Slutsky is watching all of us."

And Slutsky held the presidency at the Admissions Commission when I was being admitted to the Union of Soviet Writers[14] in 1976. Five years before that he reviewed my poetry in *Komsomol'skaya pravda*:[15]

"Kupriyanov unites Russian poetic tradition with the school of Brecht."[16] At the Admissions Commission, he identified me as an "epigone of Brecht" and a polemicist who, in his articles, tramples upon unprotected Voznezensky,[17] saying that the latter does not appear to be the secretary of the Writers' Union. Kozhinov[18] replied to him, saying that I trampled with my feet Rozhdestvensky[19] as well, who does appear to be the secretary of the Writers' Union. Then it was Tomashevsky's[20] turn, who noted that I was being accepted as a translator and not as a critic. And Slutsky agreed with that, since he had nothing against translators. The next day at the Writers' Central House, one of the colleagues hurried to greet me: "Congratulations! Yesterday, I met Slutsky and he said: I accepted Kupriyanov into the Writers' Union." That's how it happened that I joined the Writers' Union before Burich, and I had to write a recommendation for him at the beginning of the 1980s. The failed admittance of Vladimir Burich went something like this:

Frontline soldier and chief officer Ivan Stadnyuk[21] stood up and said: "This man should not be admitted. After all, Burich had been to Yugoslavia,[22] in Belgrade, and there a renowned Slavist Milivoj Jovanovich lamented how for a long time Burich was not allowed to travel to Yugoslavia." Burich did not refute. The only writer on the Admissions Commission responding to this was Irina Ogorodnikova:[23] "And why refute if he really was not allowed to go?" Then they began to find fault with the recommendations. Who? Fazil Iskander![24] Why, that one is from Metropol![25] Who else? Kupriyanov! And that one is also from Metropol. Burich was denied. But soon it was determined that Burich had not been in Yugoslavia, after all. In fact, it was I who had been in Belgrade where Milivoj Jovanovich told me in a conversation: "Too bad Volodya could not come to the October meeting." I did not argue with our old friend Ivan, but nearby stood a well-known lady writer and a good friend of the now-deceased Stadnyuk. Later she swore that she had not meant anything harmful with her report; it was simply that her popular lady poet Yu. M.[26] had "pumped her up." In the end, Stadnyuk apologized to Burich, but Iskander's and my recommendations had to be substituted by more reliable ones.

In free verse Burich saw poetry in its clear form, not clouded with formal requirements. The necessity to keep meter and rhythm creates an aberration in the author's intent, and leads to the author's unexpected result, as if deceiving the reader with limited attributes of language "sounds." I consider free verse to belong between poetry and prose: one may define it as an artistic text, symmetrical to prose in relation to poetry. It is the third type of literary writing; in ancient times it was represented by sacral writing (prayers, psalms, hymns, mantras).

As a non-religious person, it wasn't necessary for Burich to relate to the word "inspiration," but he insisted on the word "non-craftiness," understanding in it something non-handicraft in principle: "At the end of the process of creating each poem, one has to have a piece that has the effect of non-craftiness. It happens or it does not happen. It is accomplished by chance. That is why the poet experiences it as a miracle. Exactly so – 'a miracle,' just as a child happens, nothing more." To his credit Burich ascribes the following: "I was one of the original members of the group studying Theory of Language at the Institute of World Literature."[27] Here is an obvious misprint – it should have been called differently – Poetic Theory. At these yearly conferences, Burich affirmed the roots of free verse in the Russian poetic system. Yuri Orlitsky[28] shocked the students, stressing that any text written in a column is free verse. Unsuccessfully, I tried to convince the theorists that free verse does not appear as a subject of prosody. They were carefully taking apart the clouds of lyrical breaths at the precise number of spherical drops (ictuses).

Burich compared conventionally rhymed verse with the French regular garden (Versailles), and free verse with the irregular English garden. But then the ideal *vers libre* would be not a garden but a forest. This would correspond to the idea of an ideal authorship; after all, the author of a forest is not a gardener but a demiurge. And in that forest, naturally, as he defined himself, "Burich is unbound." But here Burich would answer not in poetic but business terms: "Today the Russian forest mostly resembles a prisoner, whom one may desecrate without penalty and quietly destroy." Is there then no concern for preservation of the forest from industrial postmodernism?

Burich agreed with me in that what we put into free verse is ethical force: "I lived my life according to the principle of having a different point of view. I think differently; therefore, I am." Burich was a poet who wrote "differently" – he quarreled with something silent but completely meaningful. In general, *vers libre* developed in spiraling form from the middle to the end of the 20th century, always objecting to something: from Soviet official hymns, idyllic lyricism, to post-Soviet parody, which already tramples on its own speech. Not comprehending such characteristics of *vers libre* is like not comprehending the beginning of philosophy, pre-Socratic, Plato's Socratic dialogues, concern for preservation of the forest from industrial postmodernism?

If Thales teaches that everything comes from water and Anaximander from air, then we – still all slaves of materialism, by no means dialectic – do not find here metaphors and aspirations to name that which is of higher calling and at which one cannot point a finger. For behind the obvious image of "water," "air," "fire" stands a non-representative soul, soul of the world, world's mind (Anaxagoras' "nous"). And if we try to turn around and simultaneously become idealists, again we will understand nothing; the soul will not become more tangible for us. It will realize itself not in an attribute; it will become a "soul" in the very word about it. And here it becomes clear and elicits sympathy for Burich's despair.

Why embrace
if one shouldn't smother

Why kiss
if one shouldn't swallow

I love to bring up Heracles' fragments as examples of "ancient *vers libre*." One has to learn how to differentiate between the philosophical power of language – for making clear the obvious that is not given in nature – (the non-corresponding organ of our feelings which would directly embrace the "Logos," "Tao," essence, spirit), and the poetic power of language, when already known words in an unknown position give the illusion of artistic discovery. Here one may bring up Professor Yuri Rozhdestvensky's[29] statement that *vers libre* is a lexical article, where the known (described) with the help of the known gives the effect of the unknown, a novelty. Here is Burich's example:

Life—
is a spark
struck by the cane
of the blind.

I do not agree with that philosophy, but I cannot but absorb the image. And there are in Burich: many such "lexical" aphorisms of not dispersing but reducing universal understanding: "Life is a continuous taking off of masks." "Glory is a prison of smiles…" and finally, *"Life is as simple as a cosmonaut's breakfast."* In a dozen of such "reduced" models one also finds an opening or a revelation of positivity and optimism in life:

Humanity
is an un-sunk land

Five billion
islands
of hope

That's already the law of Burich, the Archimedes; I remember how the author changed higher numbers, reaching the highest number of the planet's population. I often cited that "law" in articles, appearing not to be afraid of the poet Burich. But it seems to me that he is more limited not in "commercial" verse, but in enlarging and extolling transiency:

A butterfly
is an agreement about beauty
having equal power
on both wings

Creating his own system of writing, Burich concentrated on the regularity of the word's moment, the speech act. In his conclusion in the first book, *Texty* 1989, called "The First Poetic Tradition" (the original title was "The Second Poetic Tradition,") he differentiated among four forms of expository content: 1) clear about clear; 2) clear about dark; 3) dark about dark; and 4) dark about clear. In general, he himself wrote about "clear" or "clear about dark." Perhaps Gennady Aigi[30] wrote "dark about dark," but that has little relation to *vers libre* and has, in Burich's consideration, completely no relation to literature in general. Rhymed verse, if it is not a direct parody, which would seem interesting, falls easily into the form of "clear about dark." In this there is lack of interest toward the heuristic part of the word. In *vers libre* speech defines its relation to itself. This does not mean that it reduces completely the lyrical question – and what about the author? Is he well or not? – simply he is well, or not well, not as a "lyrical hero," but as an inquisitive subject of humanity.

But one cannot write many such instructions. One shouldn't write a large number of "living" *vers libre*. Burich wrote less than possible, only two books. Why? In his *Notebooks* we find a list of contradictory explanations. "Creative work needs intolerance, and life is tolerance. That's why one creates in youth, and lives peacefully in mature years." The bulk of his work was written "in youth" in the 1950s and 1960s. These pieces make up the first publication during his lifetime – *Stikhi* – beautifully expressed complaint. After all, on the topic of complaints one can produce only a book of complaints. "Don't write if you don't feel like it. I simply did not write when I did not feel like it." That's all good, but why does one write? And why does one not write? "I have a continuous fear of writing something poor." I know that feeling well. But here is something even more serious. "I was always afraid to write against my state and the people." This is itself very serious. He said about himself: "…I was sentenced to a higher level of literary punishment: 27 years of non-publishing." And yet, he considered himself, carefully, to be a citizen of the state and, perhaps completely in the spirit of Pushkin,[31] thought about the people.

Now, it's not important to consider what state and what people – this sounds pompous and un-contemporary. Now they hold receptions for those who "can harm" even more. Recalling Pushkin's "poet's words are the essence of his work," one understands how far from this are many popular contemporaries who make literature in order to murder words. Burich left the editorship of the journal *VOUM*,[32] finding in it a vulgar taste, in part, a gloating appearance of vulgarity in verse. In his daily speech, Burich did not curse nor do the majority of educated people, who also have good control of the language. The poet Victor Krivulin,[33] interviewed by some paper in the role of an expert, defended cursing since during debates in kitchens of Leningrad even academicians were known to use curse words. It has been long since I lived in Leningrad, and I very rarely stay in St. Petersburg,[34] so I looked over the correspondence of their academicians D. Likhachev[35] and M. Alekseev[36] and found no curse expressions there, nor in their work. The kitchen – a very important place for Russian culture!

Strangely, Burich was not published, but he carefully studied the "direction" of the journal or almanac, where they suggested he publish. But more than this, in his notes we find evidence of his fear of being published in general. Again fear, but now not of heights or small places (he adored the wide-open space of a book, but not less than a closed one), but fear as a creative principle. "Imagination is fear's sister. Fear is a brother to imagination."

I often recall the words of Spinoza who somewhere once said – wisdom is truth in thinking about life, but not death. For Burich it was the opposite. He told me with such emotion as for a student: "Slava, there is no God!" There was no fear of God in him. Instead, there was a creative fear of death. If only there would be fear of creative death! Note that a good third, if not half, of his verse is about death.

"*I entered a glue-smelling dead end*" (about a book.)

When I'll Be as Old as Earth (title of the book published in Yugoslavia for which he received a literary prize there.)

"*What are you like death?*" (that's a comparison with sleep.)

"*I am fulfilling my death number*" (that's about the process of creativity.)

"*But there is no world of adults – there is a world of the dead.*"

And the most noble one:

"*So why am I afraid to die*
if I lie down to sleep with a prayer
that everyone outlives me."

This is from the first book published while he was alive. Reading the book published posthumously, I find myself feeling that it was already written by a dead man.

"*Life is a time free from death.*"

"*Having cut my throat on a fence*
with a dim glance
I swung to the stony road of heaven."

"White marble labyrinths of heaven."

"Among the deceased
by touch
I'll find my face."

"Only death deserves verse."

"The dead
push with their feet
against the fence of the cemetery."

He loved cemeteries very much, but without any feeling of sadness. Even his home on the Oka River was his own cemetery, as he showed us the place in the ground where his ashes will be placed. In Dubrovnik we got lost in a Croatian cemetery where he, elated, described the basis of grave-stones. At that time two men entered the cemetery through the door, dressed in black tuxedos with violin cases under arm. Having heard that we speak Russian, they asked: "Is this a Catholic cemetery?" "Yes, this is a Catholic cemetery," answered Burich in a business-like manner, "and you, of course, are looking for a Jewish cemetery; the Jewish cemetery is over there," and he pointed beyond the wall where there actually was a Jewish cemetery. "Why do you think we are looking for a Jewish ceme-tery?" the musicians asked. "Well, you came with violins, so it seems you want to play at a funeral," suggested Burich. The musicians said nothing, turned around and left. Later we saw a poster of the Bolshoi Theater's symphony orchestra that was touring in Dubrovnik.

We were walking on Partisan Street in Kuntsev[37] when a woman with a brick wrapped in a newspaper came toward us. Burich froze and, in a voice of a Moscow city dweller, asked: "And where did you get a brick?" The frightened woman answered: "I am taking it to my husband's grave. When you die, your wife will do the same for you."

And again a desire to look at myself
through the bullet hole.

In his *Notebooks* we find: "*To live means to be dying, To be dying is to be alive.*" Finally, "*To dream about death until death.*" And what he dreamed happened to him. In a strange way these two events happened almost simultaneously: the long-awaited publication of his first book (I almost had to drag him by force to "Sovetskii pisatel"[38] with his manuscript) and his first stroke. He barely survived a clinical death (in 1987 or 1988), but his "fear" found some embodiment. After that, while doing an interview with radio Svoboda, I asked him about those individuals who openly harmed him. While earlier he loved to wash the ears of his enemies, he answered curtly. "I forgave them all." No doubt his relationship to God also changed. If earlier he expected from the next day only "newspapers," now there appeared something else.

CHRONICLE

Yesterday as always
I awaited
the arrival of Christ

This turnaround had to do with re-examination and the "theory of adaptation," a theory of human ability which he considered his baby and adored it, not less than *vers libre*. The theory worked better under socialism, which, by the way, Burich never rejected. Then, literature seemed one of the views of "social adaptation" and lawfully was supported by the government: "Literature is one of the branches of Russian national industry." But with Perestroika,[39] Russian national industry collapsed. Burich could not accept that. During the last year of his life he began to re-read Marx.

From the "theory of adaptation" one may conclude that the citizen overwhelms the ideal adaptability. The late Burich contradicts this:

"The citizen does not have the conviction and practices a philosophy of his own needs. To implement 'democracy' means to implement the power of the citizens. We cannot win over capitalism if it reflects the ideals of the people: vices of wealth and hedonism." And further on, "Democracy is a well-organized fraud. Bourgeois democracy is stealing from the people in the name of the people. And on that, one needs to say, is based the corresponding literature: mass literature for the spiritual theft of the people, and elite postmodernism for the spiritual degradation of the intelligentsia."

But neither does Burich see the ideal in socialism, which he tried to perfect (he had another line of work, the defense of the author's rights), and during which they did not acknowledge him, but which, according to his thinking, will return with the rise of mass population. "Socialism was rejected because it could not serve the client. And the client is always right. Socialism could not create a new man, but it made a new petty bourgeois, a new world-eater – a mutant."

I am sorry the reader has no access either to Burich's enlightened views or errors. In the bookstore Moscow, a salesperson picked up his book by its wing as though it were a sickly bird. She almost cried out: "And this is poetry!" I see progress in this, because while he was alive, some did not even consider his work to be poetry.

As a supporter of the theory of adaptation, Burich could not avoid coming to self-rejection of life. Logic was one of the most powerful sides of Burich, the poet. Some literary critics grouped our work in a class of "logical *vers libre*." I don't know whether Burich would now be able to publish openly his black "theory" that: "Man is not an organism of self-knowing nature (what for? that would be mysticism), but one of the forms of its self-destruction. The earth's cancerous tumor. (Ahead of us all is death, and we don't risk a thing)."

In one poem which may be considered his testament, he departs from adaptation, repudiates in antithesis the polar abilities of adaptation, and from customary logic comes to a logic that seems almost Buddhist:

I am
calm and sober
as an anatomy atlas
standing next to history of philosophical study
having come to the conclusion that
to be powerful is as vulgar as to be weak
to be rich is as vulgar as to be poor
to be brave is as vulgar as to be cowardly
to be happy is as vulgar as to be unhappy
to put hands on something is as vulgar as to keep them in one's pockets
I beg you
consider I did not exist

There is something Rozanov-like paradoxical in this. Besides, some of Rozanov's[40] writing may be interpreted as *"vers libre."* I translated this poem into German and stumbled on the word *vulgar*. Russian vulgarity has its history; in other languages it is less offensive. For some, these poems may seem to be an example of "negative objectivity" of *vers libre*, departure from one's own personality, in that a general poet distances from his "I." It would be strange if the author were reading a similar text, pathetically gesticulating from the stage. But disappearance of the persona does not indicate the disappearance of the creator. "Life is like reading." "Death is a condition in which one may influence, but one mustn't act."

I tried to portray Burich, but let others make corrections and, in Burich's very own words, "Everything written by one person about another is a lie."

Vladimir Burich wrote the following about himself: "I was born on August 6, 1932 in Aleksandrovsky-Grushevsky district located on the lands of former Voiska Don, in the city of Shakhtersk in East Russia, part of the Donsky basin, in a city, where my grandfather, on my mother's side, Mikhail Pavlovich Danilchenko, was a teacher. But I consider Kharkov[41] my place of birth, a city in which my mother and father met, having arrived to that city to work as chemical engineers on a project for the Giprokhim Institute.[42]

"In Kharkov, I spent the years of my childhood and youth up to age of 20, with the exception of three years for military service, from 1941 to 1944, which were spent in evacuation in the city of Chelyabinsk in the Urals. In autumn of 1953, in connection with all Soviet reorganization of the training of journalists, and moving journalism sections from philological to now independent departments, I transferred in the fourth year to the School of Journalism at Moscow State University, named after Lomonosov,[43] which I completed in 1955" (*Teksty*, Moscow: Soviet Writer, 1995, p. 322). In his *vers libre*, published after his death, we find yet another autobiographical reference:

In infancy
I was abducted by the gypsies
For meat

At seven I suggested
Making pockets on wooden shields
In order to carry in them stones
The troops of the neighboring street
Were defeated

At 11
Hiding in the trenches
From the hour of death
At the shores of a reservoir
I was overwhelmed
Having seen for the first time a woman's body

The rest will become known to you
From the published facts
Of my unpublished book

Biographical facts (*Teksty*, 1995, p. 46)

The theme of the "unpublished" book troubled him his whole life. Working as an editor in the publishing house *Khudozhestvenaya literatura*,[44] and then in *Molodaya gvardia*,[45] he published primarily his translations of poetry from other Slavic languages that he knew. These were such well-known authors as the Czech: Vilém Závada and the Poles: Tadeusz Różewicz, Marian Gzheshchak, and Tadeusz Śliwiak. He was awarded a medal by the Polish Ministry of Culture. His road to publishing was obstructed after the following poem which today seems completely "inoffensive."

The world is being filled
By post-war people
By post-war things

Among the letters
I found a piece of pre-war soap
I did not know what to do
Wash up
Or cry

Pre-war era
Is a sinking Atlantis
And we
Survived by a miracle

Frontline soldier David Samoylov did not like it, and a satirical article appeared in *Pravda*:[46] "Jobless clamber onto the Parnassus..."

Some of his free verse I quickly included in some of my articles in *Voprosy literatury*[47] and *Literaturno obozrenie*,[48] sometimes together with mine, as a result of which some of my poems ("We will play war…"), published later in schoolbooks, were attributed to Burich. He was able only rarely to publish in Moscow yearly publication *Den' poezii*,[49] beginning in 1966, when an introduction to his selections was written by the then-famous Nâzim Hikmet.[50] *Unrhymed verse appeared almost alien among the general stream of rhymed* verse:

To academician A. I. Alikhanyani

Take off the bindings of what I've seen
Take off my arms the chains of what I've done

O that first lake
reflecting the first cloud

He called himself poet-Whitmanist, follower of Walt Whitman, cultivating free verse which was new for that time. He did not support the term *vers libre* (since it is not in Russian), but was one of its first theoreticians. His first article on this topic appeared for discussion "Of What is Free Verse not Free," published in the journal *Voprosy literatury* No. 2, 1972, under the title "Of What Is Free Verse Free." That article convincingly criticizes the possibilities of traditional rhymed verse, as follows: "The sense of verse in large part depends on rhyme generating ability of the writer, i.e., rhyme appears in quality as the stimulant and regulator of associative thinking… That's why conventional poets love to call their creative process 'witchcraft,' 'shamanism,' 'magic,' 'inspiration,' and so on."

The first collection of Vladimir Burich's poetry appeared in French, translated by Léon Robel[51] in 1976, followed by a translation into Polish in 1978 (in the series "Humanum est," a literary publisher in Krakow) and in Yugoslavia in 1988. These publications contributed to his reputation as a literary "dissident." Only by the end of the 1980s did free verse begin to draw closer to the Russian, then still Soviet, reader. In 1988, the first collaborative collection of free verse poets appeared, *White Square* (Moscow, Prometheus: Vladimir Burich, Karen Dzhangirov, Vyacheslav Kupriyanov, A. Turin). The publication was a noticeable event in literary life of Moscow since the publication of this book was accompanied by several days of exhibitions and sales. In that same year, Vladimir Burich became one of the organizers of the First Festival of Free Verse in Leninsk-Kuznetsky.[52] In 1989, he received an international literary award in Yugoslavia: The Golden Key of Smederevo.[53] In the same year there appeared in Moscow a new anthology of free verse, *Time X* (Prometheus, 1989). In addition, the publisher "Soviet Writer" issued his primary book *Teksty, Stihi, Deuterons, Prose*. By deuterons he identifies the minimal poetic genre – one line (monoverse), for example:

"*Is it possible to tell a flower it is ugly?*" *Teksty*, p. 31.

"*Life is simple like a cosmonaut's breakfast.*" *Teksty*, p. 108.

By prose he meant his scholarly articles, the first of which is "Typology of Formal Structures of Russian Literary Text" which still has not been adequately evaluated by scholars, although he was a diligent participant at many poetry conferences at IMLI. His original manifesto, "The First Poetry Tradition," initially called "The Second," but then he came to the conclusion that free verse stands at the very beginning of poetic creativity. Here he supposes – "From the point of view of aesthetics, conventional poetry appears as a concrete expression of an artificial category..., and free verse – as an aesthetic category of the "natural." And further, "a general hidden dream for both conventional and free verse poets appears to be making verse in which rises the effect of non-handicraft, non-craftiness, non-artificiality, but that happens very rarely. And I aspire to that." *Teksty*, (p. 169).

Vladimir Burich died on August 26, 1994, during Struga Poetry Evenings in Macedonia. Through his widow's efforts, the poet and translator Muza Pavlova, his *Teksty, Book II, Poems, Paraphrases, Notebooks*, was published in Moscow by Soviet Writer in 1995, with an afterword by Vyacheslav Kupriyanov. This book contains almost all of his unpublished material, including earlier emotional rhymed verse. The majority of the texts, as the earlier ones, are lyrical and philosophical miniatures: "That about which only I know and about which no one will ask me." Unfortunately, that book was practically unavailable for purchase. That is why it makes sense to mention it, along with the only book that was published during his lifetime, which now seems so long ago.

Translated from the Russian by D.C.N.

ENDNOTES TO "BURICH UNBOUND"

[1] Struga Poetry Evenings – An international poetry festival held annually since 1962 in Struga, Macedonia. Skopje is the capital of Macedonia.

[2] The Metro system in Moscow closes at 1 a.m. Dinamo Metro station is just before Sheremetyevo airport.

[3] Dubrovnik – A historical town on the southern tip of the Croatian coastline.

[4] Budva – A town in Montenegro, not far from Dubrovnik.

[5] Volodya – Diminutive form of the first name for Vladimir Burich.

[6] Slava – Diminutive form of the first name for Vyacheslav Kupriyanov, poet, fiction writer, and translator who, along with Vladimir Burich, worked on developing free verse in Russia from the 1960s on.

[7] Avro Mets – Soviet poet of Estonian origin, mostly writing free verse in Russian (1937-1997).

[8] Boris Slutsky – Soviet poet (1919-1986).

[9] David Samoylov – David Samuilovich Kaufman, Soviet poet of the post-World War II era (1920-1990).

[10] Pavel Maksimovich Toper – Literary critic and member of the editorial board for the journal *Иностранная литература* (*Foreign Literature*).

[11] Andrei Yakovlevich Sergeev – Russian writer and translator of English literature, works by T.S. Eliot, W.H. Auden and Robert Frost (1933-1998).

[12] Dol'nik – The dol'nik occupies an intermediary position between the syllabo-tonic and the pure tonic systems of versification.

[13] Nikolai Trofimovich Fedorenko – Secretary of the Soviet Writers' Union board and Editor-in-Chief, 1970-1988, of the journal *Foreign Literature* (1912-2000).

[14] Union of Soviet Writers – Writers' Union of the Union of Soviet Socialist Republics was founded in 1932. U.S.S.R., also known as Soviet Union, was organized in 1922 and existed until 1991. The Writers' Union operated a publishing house Sovietskii pisatel's (Soviet Writer), and managed several periodicals, including the leading Soviet literary journal *Novy Mir* (*New World*).

[15] *Комсомольская правда* – *Young Communist League Truth*, official voice of the Komsomol, Communist Youth League, founded in 1925.

[16] Bertolt Brecht – German poet, playwright, and theater director (1898-1956).

[17] Andrei Andreyevich Voznesensky – Soviet/Russian poet whose work was translated into English by W.H. Auden (1933-2010).

[18] Vadim Valerianovich Kozhinov – Soviet literary critic (1930-2001).

[19] Robert Ivanovich Rozhdestvensky – Soviet poet who, along with a handful of other poets, pushed for a newer style of writing during the 1950s-1960s (1932-1994).

[20] Boris Viktorovich Tomashevsky – Russian literary theoretician and historian (1890-1957).

[21] Ivan Fotievich Stadnyuk – Soviet prose writer and Secretary of the Soviet Writers' Union (1920-1994).

[22] Yugoslavia – Socialist Federal Republic of Yugoslavia, founded in 1945 and led by Josip Broz Tito until his death in 1980. Thereafter, the umbrella name began to lose its members to independent states until the term dissolved in 1995.

23 Irina Ogorodnikova - President of the Translation section of the Soviet Writers' Union.

24 Fazil Abdulovich Iskander − One of the best- known Soviet writers with roots in Abkhazia. Recipient of numerous awards, he died in 2016.

25 Metropol − An unofficial literary almanac of 1979.

26 Yunna Petrovna Morits − poet and translator of foreign poets into Russian. She is most identified with the group of poets from the 1960s generation. She was born in 1937 in Ukraine.

27 IMLI − Gorky Institute of World Literature in Moscow (Институт мировой литературы имени А. М. Горького).

28 Yuri Orlitsky − Poet and Doctor of Literature, Russian State Humanities University.

29 Yuri Rozhdestvensky − Russian rhetorician, linguist and educator who founded a school of cultural studies at Moscow State University (1926-1999).

30 Gennadiy Nikolaevich Aygi (also rendered as Gennady Aigi) − Chuvash poet and translator (1934-2006). In 1993 he was named the Golden Wreath Poet Laureate at Struga Poetry Evenings in Macedonia.

31 Pushkin, Alexander Sergeyevich − The greatest Russian poet and founder of modern Russian literature (1799-1837).

32 *VOUM* − Poetry journal published during the 1980s in the city of Kaluga. Its name is based on Velimir Khlebnikov's neologism ВОУМ − from *во ум*.

33 Victor Borisovich Krivulin − Russian poet and critic, who was very active in samizdat productions and was an active campaigner for democracy (1944-2001).

[34] St. Petersburg – The city known as Leningrad during the Soviet period.

[35] Dmitry Sergeyevich Likhachev – Soviet Russian scholar, literary historian and expert in Old Russian language (1906-1999).

[36] Mikhail Pavlovich Alekseev – Soviet literary critic and academician interested in comparative literature (1896-1981).

[37] Partisan Street in Kuntsev – A district in Moscow.

[38] Sovietskii pisatel' – Soviet Writer, a publishing house of the Writers' Union of the U.S.S.R., founded in 1934 in Moscow.

[39] Perestroika – A term incorporated during Gorbachev's era of reforms in the 1980s.

[40] Vasily Vasilievich Rozanov – Considered one of the most controversial Russian writers and philosophers of the pre-revolutionary period (1856-1919).

[41] Kharkov – A second-largest city in Ukraine.

[42] Giprokhim Institute – ГИПРОХИМ, State Institute for Preparation of Chemical Reagents in Kharkov, Ukraine.

[43] Mikhail Lomonosov – Russian scientist and writer, founded the oldest and largest university in Moscow in 1755, Moscow State University, named after its founder.

[44] Khudozhestvenaya literatura – Fiction Literature, Russian publishing house.

[45] Molodaya gvardiya – Young Guard, Russian publishing house.

[46] *Pravda* – *Truth*, Russian political newspaper, established during the pre-World War I period. It was the leading newspaper of the Soviet Union.

[47] *Voprosy literatury* – *Problems of Literature*, an influential academic publication in the field of literary studies, founded in 1957.

[48] *Literaturnoe obozrenie* – *Literary Review*, a monthly magazine of literary criticism and bibliography. The organ of the Writers' Union of the U.S.S.R., published since 1973 in Moscow.

[49] *Den' poezii* – *Day of Poetry*, an annual almanac, published since 1956 by the publishing house Sovetskii pisatel' (Soviet Writer) and includes primarily poetry by contemporary poets who live in Moscow.

[50] Nâzım Hikmet – Turkish poet (1902-1963).

[51] Léon Robel – Author of many books of translations into French, among them Russian works by Gennady Aigi, Vladimir Burich and Aleksandr Solzhenitsyn.

[52] Leninsk-Kuznetsky – A city in southwestern Siberia, one of the main coal mining centers of the Kuznetsk Basin.

[53] The Golden Key of Smederevo – Poetry award given at the Smederevo Fall Poetry Festival in Smederevo, Serbia.

Translator's Note:

Soviet Union – Union of Soviet Socialist Republics (USSR) – organized in 1922 and existing until 1991, when the umbrella name gave way to 15 independent states of the former Soviet Union.

Reflections on Free Verse

by Arvo Mets

from *In Autumn Forests*

The foundation of genuine poetry lies upon a moral beginning, without which the edifice would be built upon sand. But it is expressed not in the shape of moral maxims or slogans but the highest genuine ideal.

Interrelation between freedom and necessity in free verse do not cancel each other; they alter each other, rise to a different level. Rejection of such important form-shaping elements of definitive verse, as meter, rhythm, melody, free verse must compensate, on the one side, with higher radiance of content, and, on the other, a sharp self-restriction, self-discipline. Organization of free verse is completely internal.

At the base of free verse lies rhythmic impulse. If there is no breathing in verse, all proclamations of truth in it are not worth a penny.

Thoughts in free verse are in great part compositional. A good free verse writer must possess an absolute pitch in everything that concerns a sense of form, proportionality.

In a successful composition of a book, each poem halloos with all the others. A good composition is like a complex system of mirrors, where the sun's rays endlessly reflect from one mirror to the other. In a poor composition, the poems "turn off" one another.

Definitive verse is always an address to the reader from some – even if not big but all the same – height, a stage, platform, and so on. Distinguishable particularity of free verse consists in that it reduces all distance between the poet and the reader. Free verse is a conversation without formality, heart to heart, and not necessarily in comfortable chairs; it is even more spontaneous on two stools or on bare ground.

Primarily because of this, free verse communicates to the reader an instantaneously intense feeling of participating in everything in the world – in nature, and in eternity, and in humanity, and in beauty.

The view of a free verse writer is simultaneously a view of a child, a philosopher, and a prophet.

Translated from the Russian by D.C.N.

VLADIMIR BURICH BIBLIOGRAPHY

Burich, Vladimir. "Of What Is Free Verse Free?" *Voprosy literatury*, Vol 2, 1972. pp. 132-140.

Burich, Vladimir. *Poèmes*. Translated by Léon Robel. Paris: National Institute of Oriental Languages and Civilizations, 1976.

Buricz, Władimir. *Wiersze/Poems*. Translated and Afterword by Joanna Salamon. Krakow: Wydawnictwo Literackie, 1978.

Burič, Vladimir. *Kad budem star kao zemlja/When I'll Be as Old as Earth*. Selected and Translated into Serbian by Mihailo Ignjatović. Niš, Yugoslavia: Gradina, 1988.

Burich, Vladimir, et al. *Belyi kvadrat/White Square*. Collaboration with Dzhangirov, K., Kupriyanov, V., and Tyurin, A. Moscow: Prometheus, 1988.

Dzhangirov, Karen Ed. *Time X: Contemporary Russian Free Verse*. Moscow: Prometheus, 1989.

Burich, Vladimir. *Teksty: Poems, Deuterons, Prose*. Moscow: Soviet Writer, 1989.

Burich, Vladimir. *Slobodni stihovi/Free Verse*. Selected and Translated into Montenegrin by Adam Puslojić. Nikšić: University Word, 1990.

Burich, Vladimir. *Stikhi/Poems*. Moscow: Muzei Sidura, 1994.

Burich, Vladimir. *Teksty, Book II: Poems, Paraphrases, Notebooks*. Prepared by Muza K. Pavlova. Moscow: Soviet Writer, 1995.

Vyacheslav Kupriyanov Bibliography / Awards

От первого лица/First Person. Москва: Современник/ Moscow: Contemporary, 1981.

Жизнь идёт/ Life Goes On. Москва: Советский писатель/Soviet Writer, 1982.

Домашние задания/Home Assignments. Москва: Молодая гвардия/ Moscow: Young Guards, 1986.

Эхо/ Echo. Москва: Современник/Moscow: Contemporary, 1988, 1989.

Стихи/Poetry. Москва: Зеркало/Moscow: Mirror, 1994.

Дайте договорить/ Let Me Finish. Москва: МГО СП России/ Moscow: MGO SP Russia, 2002.

Лучшие времена/Избранная лирика/ Better Times:Selected Lyrics. Москва: Молодая гвардия/Moscow: Young Guards, 2003.

Ода времени/ Ode to Time. Москва: Новый ключ/Moscow: New Key, 2010.

Ничто человеческое/ Nothing Humane. Москва: Авторская книга/ Moscow: Author's Book, 2013.

Противоречия/ Contradictions. Москва: Книжный дом/Moscow: Book House, 2019.

1986 Laureate of the Gonnesa Poetry Festival, Italy
1987 Laureate of the European Literary Award, Yugoslavia
1988 European Literature Prize, Yugoslavia
1999 Macedonian Rod of Poetry
2006 Branko Radičević Prize, Serbia
2010 Bunin Prize, Russia

2011 Mayakovsky Prize, Moscow
2012 Poet of the Year, Russia
2017 European Atlas of Poetry
2017 Felix Romulana, Serbia
2018 Yugra Prizes, Khanty-Mansiysk, Russia
2018 Naji Naaman Literary Prizes, Japan

WEST SLAVIC BIOGRAPHIES

Drago Ivanišević was born in the city of Trieste on February 10, 1907. After finishing high school in Split in 1926, he completed studies in literature and afterwards traveled and spent time in France and Italy, where he became acquainted with modern theater, poetry and art. He taught in schools in Zagreb and Karlovac, and ended his career as a professor at the Theater Academy in Zagreb. He is primarily a poet whose poems were mostly written in free verse. He died in 1981.

Janko Polić Kamov was born on November 17, 1886 in Pećine near Sušak, not far from Rijeka, Croatia. By the age of 15, he became a rebel. He attended high school in Zagreb, had a liking for music, politics, and travel. In 1906 he began to live for writing and is the first futurist in then Yugoslavia. He died young, on August 8, 1910, in a Barcelona hospital, leaving behind a few but significant pieces in both poetry and prose.

Jure Kaštelan was born on December 18, 1919, in Zakučac near Omiš. He completed his high school studies in Split and graduate studies in Slavistics in Zagreb, obtaining a Doctorate in 1955. He spent several years in Paris where he taught Croatian at the Sorbonne. Until he retired in 1980, for many years he was the head of the Department of Literary Theory. His poetry is expressionistic and surrealist which influenced the development of Croatian poetry after World War II. He died in Zagreb on February 24, 1990.

Slavko Mihalić was born in 1928 in Karlovac, Croatia. After finishing high school, he moved to Zagreb where he first worked for a newspaper, publishing his first book *Komorna muzika/ Chamber Music* in 1954. Then he worked as an anthologist, publisher, editor, critic, and writer for children, and established several literary journals, among them *Most/Bridge*. He authored more than 20 books of poetry and received numerous awards. One of the giants in Croatian literature of the second half of the 20th century, he died in 2007.

Born on April 10, 1922, on the island of Zlarin near Šibenik on the Dalmatian coast, **Vesna Parun** published her first poem in 1932 and her first book of poetry right after World War II in 1947. The book represented a new voice that deviated thematically and stylistically from the conventional literary model of the time. Free verse and colloquial expression confirmed her strictly personal style. Poet, prose writer, critic, translator and artist, Vesna Parun published numerous books and received many literary awards, and she is the first woman in Croatia who lived for and by writing. In one of the interviews conducted in the 1980s, she remarked that she had never in her work complied with external pressures, but admits complying with an inner creative pressure which she called her only tyrant – the sonnet. She died in 2010.

Antun Branko Šimić was born on December 18, 1898, in Drinovci in Hercegovina. His talent for poetry was discovered while in high school, and he published his first poem in 1913. While still in school, he introduced free verse to Croatian literature in December of 1917. His most significant collection, *Preobraženja*, was published in 1920. He continued to publish for the next few years and died of tuberculosis in Zagreb in 1925.

Dragutin Tadijanović was born on November 4, 1905, in Rastušje near Slavonski Brod. After high school he began studying forestry in Zagreb, but then moved on to study literature and philosophy, obtaining his diploma in 1937. He taught at the Art Academy in Zagreb, worked as an editor and issued many editions of Croatian writers. His poetry and prose were published in numerous collections, many of which were translated into foreign languages. He died in 2007.

Augustin (Tin) Ujević was born on July 5, 1891, in Vrgorac near Imotski. At the University of Zagreb he studied Croatian language and literature, philology, and philosophy. He traveled throughout his life, spending most time in Zagreb, Belgrade and Paris. And it is in Paris where he wrote some of his best-known poems such as "Everyday Lament." He returned to Zagreb in 1919, and two years later he began to sign his name as Tin. He began publishing in 1909 and is one of the most talented and important Croatian poets who brought depth and new lyrical forms to Croatian poetry of the 20th century. He died on November 12, 1955.

East Slavic Biographies

Born in the Chuvash Republic on August 21, 1934, and living in Moscow, **Gennady Aigi** became the most celebrated Russian poet during his lifetime. His career began by translating French poetry into Chuvash, while his own poetry was not being published in Russian periodicals or sought by Russian publishers. However, in 1984 his book of poems in French translation *Veronica's Notebook* was published in Paris, and then two books of his translations were published in English. He received numerous awards, among them the Golden Wreath of Struga, the French Academy Translators' Award, and the Andrei Bely Prize for Poetry in 1987. He was also a recipient of the first Boris Pasternak Prize issued in the year 2000. He died in 2006.

A poet, prose writer and artist, **Gennady I. Alekseev** was born on June 18, 1932, in Leningrad. He graduated from the Engineering Institute, where he later taught art history. He began writing *vers libre* as early as 1953, being the first to introduce the style in then Leningrad. From the early 1960s on his work was being published officially and unofficially in samizdat. Acknowledged as the patriarch of St. Petersburg's free verse, he is the author of six books of poetry and prose. He died in 1987.

Eugene A. Braychuk was born in 1948 in Podmoskovye, Russia. He studied law at the University of Karsnoyarsk and worked in many different fields, as a cinematographer, pianist, and marksman. A good part of his life he spent in Moscow where his work was published in *Время X* (*Time X*), 1989. He also published under a pseudonym "Стих Верлибров," *Poetic Motto*: metaphors, miniature. Moscow: Reglant, 2005.

Vladimir Petrovich Burich, known as a "literary dissident," was born on August 6, 1932, in Kharkov, Ukraine. He completed his studies in journalism at Moscow State University. Author of numerous articles on prosody and translation, he is responsible for developing free verse in post-Stalinist Russia. Burich is Russia's Whitmanist who died in 1994 while attending Struga Poetry Evenings in Macedonia.

Dmitry Grigoriev, poet and prose writer, was born on September 5, 1960, in Leningrad. He attended Chemical College of the Leningrad State University and held various positions during the course of his writing career, including that of a journalist, copywriter, and editor. He is the author of numerous books of poetry and prose, and his work has been translated into several European languages. He lives and works in St. Petersburg.

Russian free verse master, prose writer, translator, and critic, **Vyacheslav Kupriyanov** was born in Novosibirsk, Russia, on December 23, 1939. He completed his studies in 1967 at the Institute of Foreign Languages in Moscow, in the department of mechanical translation and mathematical linguistics. He has translated Austrian and German poets, Rilke, Hölderlin, and Novalis among others, as well as American poets, Walt Whitman and Carl Sandburg. He had to wait until 1981 to see his own first collection of poetry appear in print in Russia, and his 10th collection was published in 2019. A recipient of numerous European literary awards, Vyacheslav Kupriyanov was named Moscow's Poet Laureate in 2012. He lives and works in Moscow.

Arvo Mets was born in Tallinn, Estonia, on April 29, 1937. He studied at St. Petersburg University and at the Literary Institute in Moscow where he spent most of his life. He worked as an editor for several literary journals and became one of the earliest proponents of free verse in Russia in the early 1960s. He translated Estonian poetry into Russian, while his own miniature poems have been translated into numerous foreign languages. Three books of his poetry were published in Soviet Russia during his lifetime. He died in 1997.

Born on June 28, 1960, in then Leningrad, **Arsen Mirzaev** is an avant-garde poet, theoretician, editor, and organizer of free verse festivals, poetry readings, and conferences in St. Petersburg. Author of some 10 books of poetry, his most recent publication *Tree of Time* was published in 2008. His poetry has been translated into English, French, Italian, Finnish, Polish, Czech and Chuvash languages. He lives and works in St. Petersburg.

Translator's Note

Most of the poems by Vyacheslav Kupriyanov in this collection come from his book *Better Times*, 2003. It is after I had a chance to meet the poet in 2008 that I began to receive some poems from him by email. In that manner, I also received the article he wrote on Vladimir Burich. Kupriyanov himself provided most of the information on Burich. As for other Russian poets, I had an opportunity to meet Dmitry Grigoriev and Arsen Mirzaev in 2010 in St. Petersburg. I have also used whatever I was able to obtain through our library services. As for Croatian poets, I have had access to their books and also had an opportunity to meet some of them during their lifetime.

I am providing a bibliography for both Vladimir Burich and Vyacheslav Kupriyanov. However, for Mr. Kupriyanov, it was difficult to ascertain when a particular poem first came out in print. This collection, therefore, does not follow any pattern as to when the poems were written or first published, nor have I attempted to follow the sequence in the book *Better Times*. Some poems appear in more than one of Mr. Kupriyanov's books. For example, "Rabbits" appeared in at least three different publications. I had access to it first in the journal *Forum* and thus left it in that group. What is important to keep in mind is that Mr. Kupriyanov's poems speak to the reader as much today as they did in the past. My focus on selecting the poems has always been on those that speak to me and urge me to render them in another tongue, so they may be read and appreciated by an ever-wider audience.

WORKS CONSULTED

Allen, Gay Wilson. "Kornei Chukovsky, Whitman's Russian Translator." *Mickle Street Review.* 9, Part 2, 1988, pp. 35-41.

Allen, Gay Wilson and Ed Folsom. *Walt Whitman and the World.* Iowa City: University of Iowa Press, 1995.

Allen, Gay Wilson, Editor. *Walt Whitman Abroad: Critical Essays.* Syracuse: Syracuse University Press, 1955.

Balmont, Konstantin D. "Pevec licnosti i zizni: Uol't Uitman." *Vesy* 7, 1904, pp. 11-32.

Время икс:Современный русский свободный стих/Time X: Contemporary Russian Free Verse. Edited by Karen Dzhangirov. Moscow: Prometheus, 1989.

Белый квадрат/White Square. Part I. Edited by Karen Dzhangirov. Moscow: Prometheus, 1988. Part II. Arkady Turin and Karen Dzhangirov. Moscow: Soviet Writer, 1992.

Bristol, Evelyn. *A History of Russian Poetry.* New York: Oxford University Press, 1991.

Burich, Vladimir. *Тексты/Teksty I.* Moscow: Soviet Writer, 1989.

Chukovsky, Kornei. *Уот Уитмэн и его Листья травы/Walt Whitman and His "Leaves of Grass."* Sixth edition. Moscow, Petrograd: State Publisher, 1923.

Čukovskij, Kornej I. *Moj Uitmen/My Whitman.* Moscow: Progress, 1969.

Cutler, Ed. "Passage to Modernity: *Leaves of Grass* and the 1853 Crystal Palace Exhibition in New York." *Walt Whitman Quarterly Review.* 16:2, 1998, pp. 65-89.

Forum. Journal of the Croatian Academy of Arts and Sciences. Nos. 10-12, 2002.

Ginzburg, Lyubov. "The Rhythm of NEP: The Fox Trot Calls the Time," *Journal of Russian American Studies*, Vol. 3, No. 1, 2019.

Hrvatska mlada lirika/Young Croatian Lyrics. Zagreb: Assoc. of Croatian Writers, June 1914.

Judt, Tony. *Postwar: A History of Europe Since 1945*. N.Y.: Penguin Group, 2005.

Kaplan, Fred. *1959: The Year Everything Changed*. Hoboken, N.J.: Wiley, 2009.

Kaštelan, Jure. *Izabrane pjesme/Selected Poems*. Zagreb: Matica Hrvatska, 2007.

Lukić, Aleksandar. "У потрази за "Временом X"/In Search of 'Time X." A Conversation with Vladimir Burich in Požarevac, Serbia, October 14, 1990. Translated from the Russian by Dragi Ivić, *Braničevo*, 37:5-6, 1990, p. 5-12.

Maney, Kevin and Dianne Rinehart. "Here comes the Bolshoi Mac." *USA Weekend*, January 26-28, 1990.

Mets, Arvo. *В осенних лесах/In Autumn Forests*. Moscow: Red October, 2006.

Mihalić, Slavko. *Sabrane pjesme/Collected Poems*. Zagreb: Naprijed, 1988.

Mirzaev, Arsen. *Стихитростъ/Verseskill*. Taganrog: Nuance, 2011.

Most/The Bridge. The Croatian literary avant-garde in The Journal of the Association of Croatian Writers, Vol. 1-2, 1997.

Nizeteo, Antun. "Whitman in Croatia: Tin Ujević and Walt Whitman" *Journal of Croatian Studies*, Vol. XI-XII, 1970-1971, pp.105-151.

Novák, Arne. *Czech Literature*. Translated from the Czech by Peter Kussi, and Edited by William E. Harkins. Ann Arbor: Michigan Slavic Publications, 1976.

Parun, Vesna. *Šum krila, šum vode/The Murmur of Wings, the Murmur of Water*. Selected by Branko Maleš. Zagreb: Mladost, 1981.

Paternu, Boris. "Slovene Modernism: Župančič, Kosovel, Kocbek." *Cross Currents* 7(1988). *A Yearbook of Central European Culture*. Ann Arbor: University of Michigan, 1988.

Поэзия второй половины XX века/Poetry of the Second Half of the 20th Century. Edited by I.A. Akhmetev and M.Ya. Sheinker. Moscow: Slovo, 2002.

Saul, Scott. *Freedom Is, Freedom Ain't: Jazz and the Making of the Sixties*. Cambridge, MA: Harvard University Press, 2003.

Scott, Clive. *Vers libre: The Emergence of Free Verse in France 1886-1914*. Oxford: Oxford University Press, 1990.

Šimić, Antun Branko. *Preobraženja i izabrane druge pjesme/Transformations and Other Selected Poems*. Zagreb: Profil, 2005.

Ujević, Tin. *Izabrane pjesme/Selected Poems*. Zagreb: Matica Hrvatska, 1996.

Visoki jablani: Hrvatska lirika 20. stoljeća/Tall Poplars: Croatian Poetry of the 20th Century. Edited by Vinko Brešić. Zagreb: Alfa, 1996.

Walt Whitman in Europe Today: A Collection of Essays. Edited by Roger Asselineau and William White. Detroit: Wayne State University Press, 1972.

Williams, C.K., *On Whitman*. Princeton, N.J.: Princeton University Press, 2010.

Zebrowski, Walter M. Rev. "Whitman in Poland." *Polish American Studies*. 19:1, 1962, pp. 57-59.

About the Cover Artist

Marko Marian teaches art at Anoka Ramsey Community College in Cambridge, Minnesota. His landscape paintings and drawings are abstract depictions of the landscape and history of the Iron Range region, focusing on the multigenerational experiences of Croatian immigrants in northern Minnesota. Honored as Outstanding Educator for 2015 by the Minnesota State Colleges and Universities Board of Trustees, Marian's work has been exhibited locally and across the United States.

About the Translator

Dasha C. Nisula is Professor Emeritus and Fellow of Lee Honors College, Western Michigan University, Kalamazoo, MI. Author of six books and recipient of IREX and NCEEER grants, and three NEH fellowships, she translates from Russian and Croatian languages. Most recent books include *Music Is Everything* (S. Mihalić) and *You With Hands More Innocent* (V. Parun). She is a long-time member of the American Literary Translators Association. She lives and works in Kalamazoo, Michigan.

ACKNOWLEDGEMENTS

First of all, I would like to thank Michael Callaghan, Publisher of Exile Editions for his interest in this manuscript, which spurred me on to complete the work during the complex year of Covid 2020. I also want to thank Elizabeth Marquart, B.M. for her willingness to read some of the very first drafts of these poems, as well as Professor Signe Denbow of Ohio University who offered to read some sections of the early manuscript. And my thanks to Conrad Hilberry, a poet and professor at Kalamazoo College, who enjoyed reading Vyacheslav Kupriyanov's poems in translation and offered numerous suggestions. I am grateful to Dr. Roxanne Panicacci for reading and sharing her comments on the final draft. Last, but not least, I would also like to express my gratitude to Marko Marian, the artist who provided the illustration for the book cover. And I am happy to acknowledge the support of the department of World Languages and Literatures at Western Michigan University for this project.

Fourteen Vyacheslav Kupriyanov's poems in my translation were first published in the following journals:

Modern Poetry in Translation, Third Series, No. 6, 2006: "Contemporary Man," "History of Mail," "Landscape with Polyphemus," "Optimistic Geography."

International Poetry Review, Vol. XXXIII, No. 2, 2007: "Fairy Birds," "Desert," "Ode to Time," "Snow."

The Dirty Goat: Literary Arts Journal, No. 17, 2007: "Translation of Poetry," "Poetry," "Oasis of Time."

Absinthe: New European Writing, No. 10, 2008: "Ecology," "Don't Frighten the Moon."

Modern Poetry in Translation, Third Series, No. 14, 2010: "Song of Odysseus"

Nine poems in my translation were first published in the book *Duet of Iron/Western-Eastern Poets in Sympathy: Poetic Dialogue*, Kyoto, Japan: Japan Universal Poets Association, bilingual edition with Yoshikazu Takenishi, May 25, 2018: "Song of the Wolf," "Song of the Tiger," "The Dancing Bear," "To the Statisticians," "Russia's Dream," "Mass Media," "Rabbits," "Anatomy Lesson," "Pity."

Eight poems that first appeared in the journals listed above were also included in the above mentioned book. They are: "History of Mail," "Song of Odysseus," "Contemporary Man," "Poetry," "Ode to Time," "Translation of Poetry," "Optimistic Geography," "Landscape with Polyphemus."

"Despot's Clay Army" was published in *The Massachusetts Review*, Spring 2021.